UNTANGLING LIVES

A PSYCHIATRIST REMEMBERS

Nathan Billig, M.D.

For my family –
I feel fortunate to be a part of it.

Untangling Lives
A Psychiatrist Remembers

©2021 Nathan Billig, M.D.

print ISBN: 978-1-66780-086-8
ebook ISBN: 978-1-66780-087-5

CONTENTS

PREFACE

Throughout my career, when someone asks me what I like about being a psychiatrist, I always say, "I love the stories of people's lives." I also love the opportunity to help my patients untangle and understand their stories – the happy ones and also the more difficult ones caused by losses, traumas, and painful relationships and circumstances. All of our lives are made up of hundreds, maybe thousands, of stories as a result of our many experiences and relationships. Some of them we hold onto as narratives that serve as patterns for the way we live – sometimes healthy, sometimes not. Therapists have life stories too, and because the work of psychotherapy is so intimate and intense, it is essential that they constantly examine their own psychological processes as they treat patients who draw on their skills and experience and challenge their vulnerabilities. The therapist's stories must also be untangled and understood so that the work of psychotherapy with his patients can be as successful as possible.

Psychiatric treatment has always been somewhat of a mystery. Once the door to the therapist's consultation room is closed, it is unclear to those outside, and sometimes also to some inside, what goes on to make it useful as a treatment for psychological problems. In this book I present some glimpses into my work as a young psychiatrist practicing psychotherapy. I describe the process of psychotherapy and try to demystify what occurs between therapist and patient. Because I stress the importance of the personal histories and life narratives of both patient and therapist as they attempt to work in psychotherapy, I start with some autobiographical material that is pertinent to my life and to my role as a physician and a psychiatrist. I also describe case studies of four patients who were in psychotherapeutic treatment with me as I participated in my own personal psychoanalysis.

I focus particularly on the issue of loss and the path toward recovery from loss, in both therapist and patient. The theme of loss is a powerful one in the life histories of most people, including most of those mentioned in this book. The effects of significant losses heal slowly and sometimes never heal completely. Our ways of dealing with loss can influence the way we grow as individuals and attempt to live life more fully. I believe, further, that the ways in which we deal with loss are often indications of our mental health, in general. I attempt to show how loss can affect the lives of therapist and patient and be a focus for successful treatment and growth. Even for those of us who demonstrate significant resilience in dealing with loss and its aftermath, there are times in our lives when we are again acutely reminded of those losses and must rely on the strengths and coping mechanisms that we learned earlier to master those moments.

Many patients approach psychotherapy with the comment, "I really don't need to be here; I am wasting your time; there are so many other people with bigger problems." These comments may be attempts to minimize or deny losses and other traumas that all of us have experienced. Facing, understanding, and working through past losses, the feelings they engender, and the narratives created around them give us opportunities to value them as life experiences and grow as individuals. Each of us has had losses and other traumas that are "big" for us.

This book is a set of memories, reminiscences, and descriptions of patients of mine, looking into the mind and history of a young psycho-analytically oriented psychiatrist/therapist as he treats people in his care. I have worked on these ideas, as a psychiatrist, for over thirty years, and began writing them down more than a decade ago. Psychiatry has evolved in recent years so that some recently trained psychiatrists, relying primarily on prescribing medications, do not use psychotherapy of any kind as a modality in their practices. Sometimes, they do not consider the importance of their own psychological narratives nor those of their patients and the complex interactions between them. The examination of my own life, and the narratives with which I lived, have been vital to my having clarity in working with patients and to my success as a psychiatrist.

In the early years of my work in the field, described in this book, and increasingly since then, effective psychoactive medications have become important tools in comprehensive treatment regimens. Although they continue to offer significant options for relief of distressing symptoms, they are not, unfortunately, panaceas for many of the psychiatric problems that most of our patients confront.

The names of most people and places described in this book have been changed to protect privacy, and some details of circumstances have also been disguised in the interest of confidentiality. I have set my story in New York City, home through my formative years, most of my education, and the beginning of my career in medicine. The clinical facts, emotional content, and descriptions of the interactions within the life stories and relationships are intact.

I am indebted to my teachers, colleagues, family members, and patients, who have shared their stories with me and taught me about psychotherapy, and about myself.

1.

THE BRONX

I sat on the curb watching the big boys play stickball in the street. The sun felt warm and welcome on my face, arms, and legs as my hands ran idly through the city silt that had accumulated at the edge of the curb – a gum wrapper, a Canada Dry bottle cap, a rusty paper clip, some gray sooty stuff, and clumps of pollen from the trees just stirring with spring. I absent-mindedly sifted all these through my fingers as I watched the big boys and hoped that someday I could play stickball as well as they did. I daydreamed about my baseball hero, Joe DiMaggio, and wished I could also be as good a baseball player as he was. A year earlier I had eaten a quarter of a pound of butter, a whole "stick" of it, in the hope of becoming as strong as Joe D. I don't know why I thought that would do it for me; maybe mostly because I was eight years old and had dreams.

It was April 1, 1950, April Fool's Day, and more importantly, it was the beginning of spring in the Bronx. It was warm enough, so, miracu-lously, I was allowed to wear short pants and a tee shirt that day. Maybe I was finally done with the baggy corduroys and flannel shirts of winter. But spring, which always was a refreshing relief from winter, this year brought worry. For weeks, maybe months, I had a "pit of my stomach" feeling; lately it seemed worse. I did not know then that that feeling would be with me, on and off, for decades to come. On that day I felt that something was *really* wrong. I wanted to know, but I also didn't want to know. The family seemed unusually glad to get me out of the house early on that Saturday morning. Maybe that's why there was no fight about the shorts and tee shirt. Usually, I was allowed to wear short pants and a short-sleeved shirt only when spring was well along, practically summer, it seemed. I wanted to get out of the house too. There were a lot of sad, worried eyes at home that morning that spring had suddenly come to the West Bronx. We were a family that did not readily talk about feelings, particularly difficult ones, so I had no idea of the magnitude of what was coming. But I was perceptive enough to know that something momentous was going to happen.

We lived in the University Heights section of the Bronx, on Montgomery Avenue, near the Park Plaza movie theater, and not far from the Hall of Fame at the old New York University uptown campus. I spent many Saturday afternoons running past and playing among the hundreds of busts of famous people, like Longfellow, Fulton, Wordsworth, and Hawthorne, whom I did not know, except from their bronze busts and what my older brother and sisters had to say about them. I saw my first movie, *Pinocchio*, at the Park Plaza just two years earlier, when I was six. I did not actually see the whole movie because I was scared when Pinocchio ended up inside the whale, and I fled to the lobby, crying. Also in the neighborhood, near the movie theater, on University Avenue, was Olinsky's Appetizing Store where we shopped a lot. I used to go there often with my mother. I can retrieve the familiar, pungent smell of the old pickle barrels, which included separate ones for sour and half-sour pickles and pickled green tomatoes. The cheeses – farmer, pot, American, muenster, and many others – gave off another set of smells, and the herrings – smoked fish like lox, sable, sturgeon, and whitefish – yet another. The newly baked breads – rye, pumpernickel, corn – which we always bought a sampling of, never made it home intact. The mounds of potato salad, coleslaw, sauerkraut, and an assortment of delicacies including special jellied candies and several flavors of halvah were laid out in abundance. I think that only the Bronx, and maybe Brooklyn, had appetizing stores. In some other places they were called "delis," but those were not nearly the same. They did not have the multitude of flavors and smells that gave the appetizing store its character. It was a great place! It was truly a whole supermarket of Jewish delicacies.

Near Olinsky's was the candy store that sold Mello-Rolls. "Candy stores" in New York, in the 1940s and '50s and maybe before that, were like luncheonettes, but they were crammed with racks filled with all kinds of candy bars, gum, mints, newspapers, magazines, cigars, cigarettes, and even some small toys. There was a real soda fountain counter with revolving stools with leather covered seats, and you could get fresh-made sodas, several basic flavors of ice cream, egg creams (a mixture of chocolate syrup, milk, and seltzer in exactly the right proportions), and all kinds of milk shakes and malteds. Everything was jammed into the too small space of the store, so much so that items were regularly falling off the shelves. I stopped there frequently, particularly for the Mello-Rolls, the barrel-shaped chocolate or vanilla ice cream wrapped in paper that unrolled into a special cone that was also barrel-shaped on the top. Somebody creative must have thought to invent it. Another of my favorite treats of those days were the half vanilla, half chocolate Breyers ice cream Dixie cups that my grandfather would buy for me when we walked on York Avenue, near his house in Manhattan.

Montgomery Avenue had rows of houses typical of the West Bronx – everyone attached to another with alleys in between every two along one side of the street and apartment houses with strange smelling lobbies and hallways on the other. I thought that the poorer people lived across the street, although we were hardly rich. My brother, Jack, told me to try to stay on our side because it was safer. What Jack said usually went with me, except for a few times when I knew he was wrong. One day, he especially hurt me. That was the day, when I was about six, he distracted me while we sat across from each other eating lunch at the kitchen table. When I got ready to have dessert, the Milky Way candy bar that had been there for me at the beginning of the meal was gone. Jack bragged about tricking me and would not give it back. Maybe it was just a normal prank of an older brother. Despite that episode, Jack, who was seven and a half years older than me, was my guardian around the neighborhood, against potential threats from some mean, bigger kids, and he usually allowed me to tag along with him and his friends. Later, when he was a student at City College, he would take me to the campus to watch his fencing team matches or to visit the college newspaper office, where he was a reporter and by his senior year, the editor in chief.

Besides Jack, who was playing stickball with his friends, Eddie and Gene, and some other fifteen- or sixteen-year-olds that day, I also had a sister, Cecile, who was about eighteen, and another sister, Lois, who was twenty. As I sat at the curb, they were upstairs in the house with my mother, father, and the maid, Viola, who took care of me a lot since my mother got sick. I was not sure what the sickness was, but it seemed bad. I knew that my mother had had an operation and that there was a bandage over her chest near where her heart was, for a long time. Sometimes I heard that her "dressings" had to be changed, and I learned that meant she needed a new bandage. While she was in the hospital, we were always supposed to tell my grandmother, when she telephoned, that my mother was "at a meeting." I wondered if Grandma had a "pit of the stomach" feeling too, hearing that my mother was suddenly going to a lot of meetings when she never had done so in the past. Grandma was smart and must have been alarmed, but she asked no probing questions. My mother seemed weak and sad since the operation, and she did not do much around the house except rest. She usually managed a smile and seemed cheered when I was around her. One night after Viola had finished cleaning up after our dinner and had gone home, I was in the kitchen while my mother was slowly drying some remaining dishes. I saw that, occasionally, she was also drying some tears on her cheeks with the dish towel. She looked tired and sad. She looked old even though she was only forty-two. Tired from that small amount of work, she sat on a chair and with tears on her milky white cheeks, she pulled me to her and hugged me pretty hard, kissing me gently on my cheek, with just a hint of a smile. Her hands, which had been soft, were now thin, almost transparent; I could see her blue blood vessels through the skin. Maybe that was from being sad, I thought, from wringing them so much. I remember other nights, before going to sleep, when I crawled onto her bed, got right next to her, stayed there as long as I could, and looked at a book as she hugged me tight. She was warm and kind of delicate. In the opening of her nightgown, I saw the bandage over her chest, and she had a smell, not a bad one, maybe even a super-sweet one. I would later smell it again in a hospital when I was a medical student. I never did figure out whether it was a smell of healing or of getting sicker.

That year, April first was also the first night of Passover, the night of the first *Seder*. That was always a big night in our family. Until I was five, we had *Seders* at my grandparents' house on East 89th Street in Manhattan where we lived on the third floor of their brownstone house. My grandmother would have specially cleaned the house, and my grandfather, a painting contractor, repainted the kitchen every Passover. At the *Seder* he would lead the chanting of the *Haggadah*, the story of Passover; we chanted along with him and enthusiastically sang the special songs. I was usually the youngest at the table, so I had to ask the "Four Questions" that introduce the telling of the Passover story.

After we moved to our own house in the Bronx, we did the *Seders* in our dining room at a big table with fancy chairs that had high carved wooden backs with red velvet upholstery. We usually had extra people there – friends or relatives. You are supposed to invite people to Passover *Seders* who do not otherwise have a place to celebrate the holiday. We sometimes invited friends of my brother or sisters whose parents might not have *Seders*. Everybody was dressed up specially. It took practically the whole night, until bedtime, to say everything in the *Haggadah* (the book of the Passover service), to tell the story of Passover, to sing the songs that are part of the holiday, and to eat a special dinner, which somehow always tasted better than any meal during the year. You were not supposed to eat anything for the rest of the night after you finished the *Seder* meal. I always felt hungry about a half hour later. I also always felt hungry in the late afternoon on *Yom Kippur* and would sometimes sneak some of those little blue plums that are in season in the fall. In those days, I did not really have to fast on *Yom Kippur* because I was not yet thirteen, but I felt guilty anyway. In an orthodox Jewish family, it was easy to find things to feel guilty about, especially if you were violating some of the many commandments. There were a lot of rules to follow that were just part of our everyday lives, but they did not feel at all oppressive, at least not in our immediate family. I loved Passover – the whole family together, the guests, the songs and ceremony, the excitement, and the meal. I liked the ideas of Passover that we talked about each year – freedom, hope, the coming of spring, and the story of how the Jews left slavery in Egypt, thousands of years ago, with God's help. "With a strong hand and an outstretched arm" he led them out of Egypt and eventually into the Land of Israel. That was always extremely exciting to me, even though we repeated it every year, actually twice each year, because *Seders* were conducted on the first two nights of the holiday.

I knew that Passover was starting that night, that April 1st, but no one seemed as happy about it as they usually were. In fact, no one had mentioned it in over a week. There was none of the usual exhilaration and excited preparations. I wondered if the dishes had been changed and if the Matzo, the unleavened bread eaten at Passover, and other special foods, had been bought. It all seemed to have been forgotten, but that, I knew, was impossible.

So, I sat on the curb watching the stickball game and, suddenly, I was called into the house by one of my sisters. I guessed that it was close to lunchtime. Then I was told **the news**. Someone, I am not sure who, said, "Nathan, Mommy died." Then they nervously and haltingly quickly added, "Mommy has gone to sleep forever; you'll never see her again." I did not really understand. Was she dead or was she asleep? At age eight, I was not sure what "dead" actually meant when you were talking about a person. I had only seen dead animals in the street; most of them had been run over by cars. I guess that if I would never see her again it did not really matter whether she was "dead" or "asleep forever." I cried and ran to Cecile who comforted me. She was crying too. She usually comforted and protected me when I needed it. My father looked stricken with sadness. Everybody around me cried. They all might have known before that day that my mother was going to die. I did not, except that is probably why I had that "pit of my stomach" feeling for weeks or months before. So maybe I did know it on some level or at least sensed the anxiety in the house. It seemed that suddenly, in an instant, I did not have a mother anymore. I did not understand then how that could happen, so fast, without warning. One second you had a mother and the next second you didn't? I guessed that the other people in the family had some warning about this, and maybe they even had a chance to say good-bye. Would I have felt better if I had a warning? Probably not.

What happened that day, after the announcement, is a little blurry, but somehow, I ended up, in the late afternoon, at the Manns' house, a few streets away, for a *Seder* with their family, while the rest of my family stayed home. I think that my Uncle Harry and Aunt Martha came to the house. I also was told that I would sleep at the Manns' that night. I did not want to be there, but I did not put up a fight about it either. I tried to be *a good boy* in the face of this huge upset in the family. I guess there was too much going on at my house. The Manns were among my parents' closest friends, and David Mann was one of my best friends. I wondered if my family was having a *Seder* at my house. I missed the family and the excitement. Maybe it was not going to be a real *Seder* there. Maybe everybody was just sitting around crying or something like that, and maybe they wanted me to have a real *Seder*. As we gathered and sat down in the Manns' dining room, a key Passover question popped into my head: "Why is this night different from all other nights?"

I felt that maybe I would not be able to take a deep breath for a long time, or maybe forever. I also had a lump in my throat. I could not be happy about Passover; why were we even having a *Seder*? I knew that you were supposed to observe the holiday, even though your mother just died or went to sleep forever. From then on, Passover would always be different for me. From then on, I thought, I would always be different. I do not remember the actual *Seder* that night. I remember that after it was over, Mrs. Mann made up the couch in the living room as a bed, and she helped me get ready to go to sleep on the couch. She hugged me; I could not fall asleep. I wondered where and how my family was; I was alone with the Manns. We could not use the telephone to call my house because the Manns, like us, did not use the phone on *Shabbat* or holidays. Was I ever going home? I felt kind of stranded. While I was lying there thinking about this terrible day, all of a sudden, I wet my pants, but I don't remember feeling like I had to go to the bathroom; it just leaked out or forced itself out. I messed up my pajamas and underpants and got the corner of the couch a little wet. I got nervous because Mrs. Mann, although nice, was also fussy about things like cleanliness. I quietly tried to clean it up myself, but it was the middle of the night. I did not know what to do with my wet underpants and pajamas. I think I put them under the couch and hoped for the best. No doubt they were later found. I think that the corner of the couch still had a stain on it the next day. I did not go to my mother's funeral. That day is all a blur, too, but I did return to my house with my family.

For the first week after my mother's funeral, we sat *shiva* at our house, which meant that all of the family sat around on small hard wooden benches in our house, the mirrors were covered, prayers were said, and friends and acquaintances, mostly all grown-ups, came to visit to say nice things about my mother in hushed conversations and to make sure we were alright. I overheard someone say that Mommy was "saintly"; I did not know at the time what that meant, but I guessed it sounded good. It did not really sound Jewish! People seemed to feel sorry for us, maybe for me because I was still a kid. Some people cried. I marveled at all the baskets of fruit and the large plants that were sent to us. Did that happen every time someone died? Amazing! It was kind of exciting, and even festive, although it was not supposed to be so. During those few days, I did not feel so bad; I liked having everyone come to the house. It was sort of like a holiday or even a party but not a happy party. I cried in my bed at night, even though not that much was so different. In her last months, my mother had rarely put me to bed; Cecile usually helped me with a shower, read to me, tucked me in, and kissed me good night. Sure, I always spent some time on my mother's bed before I went to my room, and I missed that. I missed just knowing that she was there. There is something about your mother that you just want her to be there, whether she is sick or well, maybe even if she's nice or not. Mine, as far as I could remember, always seemed nice, but she was sad much of the time in the last months of her life.

For the weeks and months that followed, we were treated differently than we had been in the past. Friends of our family and people in the neighborhood sent lots of food to the house. After the first week, the week of *shiva*, we were invited to people's houses for dinner practically every night for a few weeks, and then on Friday nights for a few months, particularly by the rabbi of our synagogue, Rabbi Kramer, and his wife, Tirza. They were probably giving us dinner because they thought we had no one to make it. They wanted to be caring, which they were, and they wanted to make *Shabbat* special. They meant well, but I felt a little freaky about it. I felt like poor people might feel who are given free meals – glad to have them, but not liking the fact that we needed them or that they felt sorry for me. I did not want the reason for their feeling sorry to have happened, and it had. Viola or my sisters could have made dinner, and they did sometimes. Gradually we managed on our own. Many years later, when I was newly separated from my wife, I felt self-conscious and rejected some well-meaning dinner invitations without fully realizing that the source of the awkward feeling then may have related, at least partially, to that time when I was eight.

It was lonely, sad, and embarrassing to have no mother at age eight. I was not sure how to say it to people. I was not able to say it to myself. I tried to avoid the whole subject of mothers as best I could, but for kids of eight or nine, mothers are, or should be, important people in their lives. "Where's your mother?" someone in a store asked, when one day I did not have the right change for a Mello-Roll. I avoided the answer and just ran out of the store without the ice cream. Salesmen coming to the front door of our house would ask, "Is your mother home?" I would say "no" and slam the door. "What happened to your mother, anyway, Nathan?" some of my friends would ask repeatedly. They knew that I didn't have a mother anymore, that something had happened to her, but I think they didn't really understand this death business either, or they wanted to see what my answers were. I would try to explain, using some of the words like "breast" and "cancer" that I had heard from the adults in the house on the day she died and during the *shiva*. The words did not really make sense to me, and my friends were mystified and scared because it seemed to them, too, that one day I just didn't have a mother anymore; it could happen to them.

A few times, walking home from school on University Avenue, near Witkin's Butcher Shop where we shopped, I saw a woman from behind walking into or out of a store. For a moment I thought, *Oh, there's my mother*, and forgetting what had happened, I would excitedly run up to the person to tell her what had happened at school that day, only to find as I got close, sometimes right up to her face, that it was not my mother after all. I really wanted her to be there. I needed her on those days, I guess, or maybe I just needed her in general. The reality of her death had not sunk in.

Then there was the whole problem of God. We grew up to believe that he was kind and that he knew everything, watched over everything and everybody, and was so powerful that he either caused everything to happen or could certainly influence anything that might happen. Having your mother die when you are eight could shake those beliefs. Even before her death, I remember always being frightened by the prayer during the High Holy Days that includes, "Who shall live and who shall die," and then it spells out the various ways, such as hunger, stoning, illness, and others, in which people can die during the next year. "On Rosh Hashanah it is written and on Yom Kippur it is sealed." That referred to your fate! "Repentance, prayer, and charity can avert the evil decree," the prayer continues – serious and very scary. Maybe my mother did not do enough of those three things last year! It was hard to believe that. She was a good person, raised in an observant orthodox Jewish family. Some of my deeply religious aunts and uncles, although also sad, explained her death and others, as they did many things: "It's God's will; we don't understand His ways; it's part of His plan." At that time of my life it seemed to me like a lousy plan, but who was I to question God? I was only a kid. I have had some trouble with those beliefs ever since. The God of the Jews seemed harsh to me that year. In later years

I was stunned, but relieved, to hear that a devout but "modern" relative of mine, whom I greatly respected, had had trouble believing in a caring and merciful God since the atrocities of the Holocaust. Nonetheless, she observed all the prescribed rituals and practices of orthodoxy because she felt that they were the essence of Judaism.

At about the time my mother's illness became apparent, I also remember having repetitive scary dreams about the occasional day trips that our family made to Bear Mountain State Park, cruising up there from Manhattan on the Hudson River Day Line boat, at least once each summer in my early years, for a day of fun away from the City. I loved those trips and remember running around the boat playing tag with other children, having special snacks, eating soggy tuna fish lettuce and tomato sandwiches on rye bread that we brought from home, looking at the lifeboats and imagining times when they might have to be used, seeing the pistons that made the boat work, and watching the land magically go by, alongside the boat, as we left Manhattan island for "the country." When we got to Bear Mountain, we played in the woods, in the playgrounds, and in the huge swimming pool all afternoon, until we were exhausted from all the fun activities and had to get back on the boat to go back to the City in the early evening. In my dreams, beginning around the time that my mother was getting sick, we were on a Hudson River Day Line boat on a bright sunny day when the boat suddenly stopped cruising and began to slowly sink into the Hudson River. As each deck was submerged, my mother and I struggled to get to the next higher deck. I was aware of the suspended lifeboats, which were hung in their places on the sides of the boat. Eventually the water reached to the topmost deck, and we were huddled together near one of the smokestacks, about to go under, when I suddenly woke up, frightened and crying but relieved to be safe in my bed at home.

2.

DR. ADLER I

D r. Marvin Adler was a big bear of a man, with a friendly face, a large wedge of a nose, a furrowed brow, a warm, friendly but cautious smile, and a meaty handshake. He was approximately six feet, two inches tall, weighed 250 pounds or more, and when he came into the waiting room from his private office, he seemed to fill the whole doorway in between. Before determining that Dr. Adler was indeed well-suited to be my psychoanalyst, I had interviewed a few other analysts as part of an arduous and highly emotional mutual selection process.

As a young psychiatrist, the decision to seek out a psychoanalyst for myself had been an anxiety-filled process of unrealistic proportions. At that time and in the psychiatric atmosphere in which I trained and practiced, it felt like a requirement "to be analyzed" in order to be an effective psychiatrist. It made sense to me that a psychiatrist should clearly understand his own past and the influences on his life before he saw patients and had to deal with their stories. I did not feel that I had a choice. Like some of my peers, I was a bit worried that I might not be "accepted" or found "suitable" for analysis, although that was unlikely. The consultation process would determine my suitability and allow me to choose an analyst with whom I felt I could work in treatment for at least several years. I wanted to find "a good fit," although it was difficult at that point to list the necessary qualifications. There was also some likelihood that I would continue in training in a postgraduate psychoanalytic institute to become a psychoanalyst. Most of the psychiatric residency programs of the 1960s and '70s already provided a very sound grounding in psychoanalytic psychotherapy, but nonetheless, many of my cohort of residents went on for several more years of postgraduate training in an analytic institute to become psychoanalysts.

I had consulted with three highly regarded senior analysts, who were referred to me by my supervisors and colleagues. Each of them had said, on the telephone, that they had or would soon have treatment time available. All were members of the faculty of the prestigious Psychoanalytic Institute, the most classical or "orthodox" institute in the City at the time. That is, the analysts associated with that institute were said to adhere, most closely, to the theory and therapeutic practices laid down by Freud or modified by his early disciples. Many were proud of basically not having changed their technique or theoretical framework very much in the thirty or so years since Freud's death. Others had somewhat modified Freud's theory and practice and had a more "modern" outlook. The most senior stalwarts of the immediate post-Freud era in New York had either died or were already quite old, so I did not consult with any of them, but there was a new cadre of admired and respected doyens.

I remember being terrified, mildly trembling, as I had entered Dr. Sidney Marks's office to begin my first venture into the world of patienthood. I felt, and must have looked, like a scared lamb being led to slaughter. Dr. Marks's office was austere with simple, old, nondescript antique furniture, little color, and long dark gray curtains drawn over a virtual wall of windows. At some point in the consultation session, I figured out, maybe to distract myself a bit from Dr. Marks, that had the curtains been opened they would have revealed a priceless view of the East River and the skyline of mid-town Manhattan, toward the UN Building. He kept them tightly closed, I thought, to preserve an excessively solemn atmosphere. I wondered why he would do that. Nervously, I skimmed through my life story of thirty-plus years and, from the start, experienced this analyst as a sadistic inquisitor, trying to probe my saddest feelings and test the limits of my memory, repression, and indeed, maybe even my sanity. I felt that he bored right in on me. For a first session, I thought he was excessively harsh; I knew that that kind of approach was unnecessary. I was gentler with my patients in the first consultation, especially if I thought I might continue to work with them in psychotherapy. I wanted to start building an alliance right from the start. I quickly realized that I was surely gentler, in general, than Dr. Marks. He seemed not to be able or want to control this aspect of his character.

Among many other things, he wanted to know the various ways I would interpret that repetitive dream of the Hudson River Dayliner boat; if and how I, as a child of eight, thought about my mother when I was told she was dead and in what ways the subsequent deaths in my family were related in my thoughts to my mother's. It was not only what he asked; it was his manner that was so off-putting, indeed bordering on abusive. He was abrupt, abrasive, and unsmiling, interrupting me frequently to move on to something else. It felt as though he was sticking a pin into me, here or there, as I was telling him intimate details of my life that I had never fully discussed with anyone else before. Somehow, he reminded me of the stereotypic interrogating German SS officers portrayed in the World War II movies of the 1940s and '50s. After the one-and-a-half-hour consultation, I felt as though I had wrestled with an angry wild animal, barely escaping with my life. I walked onto bustling Third Avenue, took a deep breath of the rather polluted New York air, and wiped the sweat from my brow.

I'll never do that again, I thought. *This is too, too hard. I'll do without psychoanalysis*, I concluded, *and somehow I'll get by.*

Maybe Marks's inquisition was a test, and my thoughts went to the Biblical Abraham, leading Isaac to his possible sacrifice; but Abraham seemed much kinder. I knew that he had to be conflicted, although he was trying to be obedient to God. Later, during my eventual analysis with Dr. Adler, I once associated Dr. Marks with my deeply religious Uncle Charlie who would test me, also rather harshly, whenever I visited his house, as a young child, on what I had learned in *cheder* (Hebrew school) that week. Much later, I discovered that Dr. Marks was, in fact, a survivor of a German work camp. I assume that he had been scarred and had freely inflicted his pain on me, and I assume others. I also heard that several analytic candidates had complained that he was unnecessarily and harshly critical in class and in case supervision.

Then there was Dr. Richards who had gone to Princeton and must have come home from there with a British accent, since he had never lived anywhere near the United Kingdom nor any part of the Commonwealth. He seemed more involved with what looked like his expensive silk tie than with me, an anxious potential patient and a future colleague. His office was furnished in what I thought were rather fancy French antiques, and from his frequent glances around the room, I imagined that he was checking that everything was in perfect order. Early in the consultation interview, I mentioned in passing that I had recently joined a health club which was on the same street as his office and just a ten-minute walk from mine. During the hour, he seemed unusually preoccupied with my membership in the health club and came back to the subject several times to inquire about the particular activities I enjoyed at the club. Then, at the end of the session, which had been rather informal, benign, and chatty, especially when compared with Dr. Marks, he said that he had time available to see me in analysis four times per week starting the next month. But, he added, that because he, coincidentally, was a member of the same athletic club, I would have to refrain from using the club during the years of analysis with him, so that we each could be assured of our privacy. I thought for a moment: "we each could be assured our privacy," but only he would have use of the health club for which I had just plunked down a $250 initiation fee. Whatever happened to *mens sano en corpora sano*? I guess the patient's *corpora sano* had to be attained somewhere where the analyst's wasn't.

Incredulous, I began to imagine the scenario of going to the management of the club to get back the initiation fee, telling them that I had to withdraw because my new psychoanalyst prohibited my attending there while I was in treatment with him. The manager of that facility would have to be an associate member of the Psychoanalytic Institute or a former patient of Dr. Richards to buy that story. More likely he would agree that, with a story like this, I certainly needed to see a psychiatrist. Maybe he would require a note from the doctor saying that my attempts to become more mentally healthy required that I withdraw from the club, and "therefore would you please return this man's initiation fee without prejudice." Maybe Richards had encountered this conflict previously and had an arrangement with the club whereby they would hold a potential patient's fees in escrow until the good doctor cured him of his neurosis. I was titillated, laughed about this new world I was encountering, but I was also discouraged. I left Dr. Richards's office, shaking my head in disbelief, and I telephoned him to decline his offer to be my analyst as soon as I reached my office. I did so, primarily, because I thought he seemed self-involved and preoccupied. (I later appreciated his concern about the lack of privacy we would both have at the health club, but I thought he handled it poorly.) He had a little trouble taking my rejection when he countered, "It wouldn't have been a good marriage, anyway." *Marriage*? I thought. That was an interesting way of putting it. I had no intention of making this a "marriage." And what if I had agreed to see him and not go to my health club? Then would the "marriage" have had a better prognosis?

I wondered if these first two analysts had available time because they were so obviously flawed that no reasonable person, and certainly no relatively healthy young psychiatrist, would subject himself to their apparent sadism, narcissism, and possibly other personality problems in the attempt to be psychoanalyzed. Wow! Did the Psychoanalytic Institute know about these guys? Someday I would let them know. I knew that a personal psychoanalysis would not be fun, but I had expected that the analyst would ease me into the still frightening process, be an ally in my efforts to better understand my life, and help me explore and resolve some of the specific issues that bothered me.

So, it was with great relief that I met with Dr. Adler, who initially and fairly continuously impressed me as a *haimish*, decent, caring, and bright man with no obvious pretensions, no concerns about health clubs, no phony British accent, no preoccupying silk ties or gray curtains hiding windows, and no apparent sadism. He appeared to be a *mensch* right from the start. He would reliably open the door at the appointed time and, with a kindly but slightly concerned countenance, and that rather constantly furrowed brow, signal for me to enter the "holy of holies," as I jokingly called his office. For the first three or four sessions, I sat in a chair facing him, and when I must have passed some preliminary test and was deemed fit for psychoanalysis, I was invited to "try the couch." I was to "try" it for the next four years, four times per week. That was a common schedule and average duration for an analysis, although the number of years on the couch was variable. Although I knew that I really was not crazy, I initially felt a surprising sense of relief that I was an acceptable candidate for this unusual process, and with a man who seemed as though he cared about people, and who also was apparently rigorous enough to be a training and supervising analyst at "The Institute," as it was called in the trade. I never did figure out how, or if, he ever related to the first two analysts with whom I had tangled. They were in a different, and definitely minor, league compared to Dr. Marvin Adler.

There were no pretenses about this man. His office was spare but comfortable, awkwardly Danish modern, with a lot of teak, the requisite psychoanalytic Persian rug (Freud had them on the floors of his consulting rooms and covering his couch in Vienna, and in Hampstead; I had visited both shrines), and a rather ordinary black leather, possibly Naugahyde, and cloth analytic couch on which he laid out the obligatory paper napkin for each new patient's head to be examined. (The napkin, to prevent soiling the upholstery and to observe an element of public health between patients, was made of cloth in some settings.) I got into the habit rather quickly. Regularly, usually at 8:30 a.m., when that tight, soundproofed door opened with a groan, I knew my time had come, and I would go in, assume the analytic position on the couch, my head resting on the newly unfolded paper napkin, and I began talking. For four years, four times per week, I would lie on the couch and talk, staring, mesmerized by the two Johnny Friedlander prints in wormwood frames on the wall in front of me. They were not particularly attractive, I thought, nor were they at all distracting. Maybe they were a good investment, like the Persian rug that did not really go with the Danish modern furniture. Dr. Adler would sit in an armchair at the head of the couch, out of my sight, of course, unless I sat up and turned around. Turning around to see if the analyst is awake, or otherwise engaged, is definitely frowned upon, but occasionally, when I felt particularly boring, or rarely mischievous, I did check on him and he always seemed OK and never asleep in his comfortable chair. "Marvin," something I called him only to my friends and colleagues, and to his face several years after I "terminated," would comment, clarify, interpret, and sometimes summarize in a gentle, thoughtful, and concise manner the "material" I presented. He used few words and expressed himself simply. Early on I thought he was being too careful with me. I began to worry. Was I so fragile? Was this how all analysts worked? I was sure that the more "orthodox" Dr. Jacobi, my teacher of psychoanalytic theory and practice during my psychiatry residency, would not be like this. He would be more of a hard-ass, or at least his interpretations would be more complex, more intellectual, abstract, and, possibly, more curative. I occasionally berated Dr. Adler for his softness. After all, I was a big boy, a smart, fully trained psychiatrist with patients of my own. I could take the rough stuff. Maybe Dr. Adler already knew me and what I needed better than I knew myself, or maybe this was just his style. He pointed out my sensitivity to being treated "too carefully" versus being treated "without care" and my talking a lot, at least initially, about analysts who were "tough" and those who were "soft."

The psychoanalytic process is a self-indulgent luxury, I thought. I would drone on, rather repetitively, maybe even boringly, about whatever came to my mind (those are the basic instructions that supposedly help make it work) – a lot of trivia of everyday life, conflicts, joys, old mem- ories, horrors, dreams, fantasies, thoughts and feelings about my life, old and new, the analyst and the process. After about forty-five to forty-seven minutes, he would often, but sometimes not, make some brief summary comments and then I would leave the office, walk through the lobby of the 87th Street apartment building that housed his office, be greeted again with a nod from the knowing doorman, and rush off, seven minutes away, to heal the patients who came to my couch-less, but somewhat better decorated, office. The doorman at Dr. Adler's building obviously had sardonically smiled at generations of analysands of the five psychoanalysts occupying the first floor of the building, as each passed through the lobby, coming and going for years. Supposedly he once had to tell the arriving patients of one older analyst that their doctor had died since the last session. Unfortunately, the analyst's family had not yet been able to contact them. You could tell by the doorman's demeanor that he saw himself as an adjunct to the analytic processes of the building. He acted like the guardian of the Temple, and maybe aspired to one day be named an honorary training and supervising analyst or possibly to be invited to move a few blocks away to become the doorman of the "The Institute" itself.

Dr. Adler's office became an unreal haven for me, a strange corner of my world. It seemed a little odd to have this private place, to trust a stranger with my most intimate thoughts, stories, feelings, secrets, deviations, indiscretions, dreams, and fantasies, but at the same time I loved it and felt fortunate to have the opportunity to do this, no matter how painful it eventually became. Dr. Adler and I established a relationship in which he expected me to be as honest as I could be in reporting what was on my mind and I expected him to be caring and smart in helping understand my psyche so I could live as free of significant conflict, anxiety, and sadness as possible. I also hoped that I could be increasingly effective in my work with patients, be a better husband, and eventually, a wise and loving parent. In sum, I hoped, especially in view of the career I had selected, that I would be an accurate observer of the patients who came to see me and know where my "craziness" stopped and others' began.

I had entered analysis with some bravado, not dissimilar from patients of mine who would say, "There are so many people who need your expertise more than I do; I shouldn't be wasting your time." I was savvy enough not to ever say that aloud to Dr. Adler. I knew that I *had to do* an analysis, but, surprisingly, I had only vague ideas about what was "troubling" me, and it was extremely hard to own up to the idea of having any "problems." I was not supposed to have problems. I had taken care of myself and some others around me for many years, maybe even going back to childhood. It seemed like a great relief now to admit to some frailties, but could I do it? It took a while just to fill Dr. Adler in on the cast of characters of my life, the family history and culture, and much more. I was slightly alarmed, right off, that he did not know what an "appetizing store" was. He had grown up in the Midwest, I thought, where apparently there were none, and now they were a rarity even in New York, yielding to big all-inclusive supermarkets. His inexperience with Olinsky's was not, however, a real deficiency; he was a quick study. He got the gist of that and other New York-type experiences from my graphic descriptions. He also got the orthodox Jewish stuff, although I had the feeling that he was a rather secular Jewish guy. He was not familiar with the Yiddish word, *schvach*, a great expression, which was used a lot in our family. It meant that something was "not so great, a bit off, just miss, not as good as expected." But, nonetheless, he was interested, patient, and waited for my story to unfold slowly; I was grateful for that. It remained somewhat scary to me that I trusted, liked, maybe even loved Dr. Adler so soon in the process. He rapidly became the idealized solid father I did not have, but had not, until then, consciously admitted that I missed. He could also be the kindly mother I knew too briefly. In contrast to those feelings, I found that I could periodically, easily, and loudly diminish his importance to me, decry the ludicrous nature of the process, and berate him for the few obvious inadequacies I perceived. Soon after starting analysis, I began to have a familiar gnawing feeling that Dr. Adler, or at least my relationship with him, would not last. I did not know if that was just my consistent and worried view of life, transference (unconsciously transferring a feeling to Dr. Adler and this situation from my past), or whether I was prescient that I would lose him before I was ready. That damn "pit of my stomach" feeling, which was so familiar to me, recurred! Of course, I told him about this feeling, and he summarized, "You fear that our relationship will end prematurely?"

"I guess so," I said, without much feeling.

———

After my two-year stint in the U.S. Air Force, I had been invited to teach part-time at the hospital where I had done my training in psychiatry, and I also planned to start a private practice. I was grateful that to have been stationed at Andrews Air Force Base, outside of Washington, DC, barely escaping being sent to the war in Vietnam. At Andrews, I examined and treated the servicemen and women ravaged by war who were being sent back to the States for treatment. I watched President Richard Nixon fly in and out of the base frequently on Air Force One, always with great pomp. Once or twice per month, even members of the hospital staff were asked to show up at the flight line and simulate a crowd of cheering, welcoming citizens. But the most arduous and painful task of my days in the air force was meeting the large C-5A transport planes, converted into giant flying hospitals, that would land at Andrews on their way back from Vietnam, via the Philippines or Japan, distributing patients to various bases and veterans' hospitals on the East Coast. In addition to our regular duties, each physician at Andrews had nights on call to "greet" the airplanes and check each patient, inspecting postoperative, sometimes gory, battle wounds and amputation stumps, evaluating changes in vital signs and mental status, and assessing other symptoms to determine whether the patients could move on immediately to more distant destinations or needed to stay over for a few days or more at the hospital at Andrews. Those were wrenching hours, every few weeks, but otherwise the two years went by quickly, especially considering where I could have been. I was grateful to be just outside of Washington, DC, rather than at Cam Ranh Bay.

Although I had matured as a psychiatrist in those first years out of training, I also became more aware of a mild, episodic anxiety that was not with me daily or even weekly but rarely missed a month. It seemed like a return or continuation of that "pit of the stomach" feeling that I had as a child since the months just before my mother died, and maybe even before that. At other times, I felt a mild sadness that might last a day or two and which I did not connect to any real events in my daily life. There was no ostensible reason for upset. I had made it so far. I had gone to good, but not world-renowned, schools. I had excelled in my training as a psychiatrist and had been invited back to teach after the time in the air force. As my tour of duty had progressed, I felt more aware of both the occasional anxiety and feelings of sadness, neither of which incapacitated me beyond rare episodes of short temper or times of excessive rigidity about how I led my life. I was usually regarded by family, friends, and colleagues to be a sensible, reliable, caring, healthy guy. I never admitted any symptoms to my wife or friends. I did not want to be weak. I wanted everything to be right, easy, with no glitches, no bad surprises.

Few of us can expect such luxuries. And certainly, that is not the way my life had been. Although I always seemed to naturally smile a lot, I probably worked harder at it than I knew. Maybe I had been generally trying too hard for too many years without knowing it; maybe I was getting weary of trying so hard to control everything in my environment. I attempted to defensively keep life's worries out of my awareness as much as possible and, as a result, was not as aware of my inner workings as I could have been. I entered analysis, in part, because I wanted to be free of the anxiety about trying so hard to keep my life so steady and to be a "good boy" all the time. I did not want to be so afraid of what might happen if I let down my guard, and I really wanted to let it down. I also had to better understand the effect of the losses in my life. I had largely put them away, but I knew they were a part of me, buried somewhere inside. Being a psychiatrist, I am sure that I also overanalyzed a lot of what other people considered trivial thoughts and feelings.

I was eager to get on with the process of analysis and was impatient whenever I felt that Dr. Adler was not working to move things along. I tried to be a good boy in analysis and do my part there, although on occasions I would be five minutes late, having dawdled over an extra cup of coffee. One time I remember that I just bagged the whole session, while I had a leisurely breakfast and read the *Times* at a diner a few blocks away and called Dr. Adler to tell him I was "caught in traffic" and would miss the session. Although I partially acknowledged them, I am not sure that I fully owned up to the deliberate aspects of those episodes until much later in the analysis. I assume that those were times when I just did not want to fully engage in the analytic process, because we were likely confronting something that I did not quite want to face, or maybe I just wanted to be *bad* to see what it felt like and what the repercussions would be. Dr. Adler let me know that he considered all these possibilities, but he did not press for clarification.

After about nine months in psychoanalysis, Dr. Adler told me that during his planned upcoming summer vacation time, he would have to spend a week in a hospital, the same hospital where I occasionally saw medical or surgical patients for psychiatric consultations. Clearly breaking with his usual analytic stance about such things, he said that he was telling me some personal details because he did not want me to be surprised if I met him in a hall or elevator there when he was supposed to be on vacation. He revealed that he had had treatment for a heart ailment several years earlier, and now needed some follow-up treatment associated with that. He assured me that to his knowledge, he did not now have a life-threatening problem. He would plan to see me in three weeks, as scheduled. I immediately felt both angry and sad. Maybe I had made the wrong choice of an analyst, I thought. I should have chosen someone entirely healthy, with whom the risk of loss would be minimal. Did analytic patients ever ask their future analyst about his medical history, before embarking on this lengthy process? Was I overreacting? This fit in with my worst fears about close relationships. Dr. Adler asked what my thoughts were about this new information. I said that I was worried about him, and about me, worried that I would lose him, but hoped that everything would work out as he described. My eyes welled up with tears; the session was over.

3.

ZLOCHEV - NOW AND THEN

exited the car-clogged Long Island Expressway and wended my way through some nearby streets of Queens until I came to the Mount Hebron Cemetery. It had just stopped snowing and the attendant at the gatehouse advised me to leave my car in the parking lot and proceed carefully on foot. I wandered through the cobblestone lanes of the cemetery. I marveled at the masses, indeed thousands, of gravestones of varying sizes and shapes. They proclaimed that a Bernstein, an Alpert, a Cohen, a Diamond, some Rosenbergs, an Epstein, several Silvermans, and so many thousands of others were buried here for perpetual care. The graves were dusted that day with clean white snowy powder, under the gray sky of Flushing, New York. Small stones placed on top of some of the grave markers, bumps beneath the snow, signaled that visitors had come in the recent past. That had not been part of our family custom, but it seemed like a sweet gesture to me. There were some gated clusters of graves which seemed to be arranged like reincarnations of towns or *shtetls*, as if transported from Eastern Europe to Queens. In fact, many of the groupings were the members of associations of *Landsleute* from the same town or village in Europe over the last hundred years. They had joined together as struggling refugees in the early part of the twentieth century, attempting to start new lives in New York, and now they and some of their children were buried together in peace in the New World.

Finally, I came to Zlochev's resting place. Startled by the sudden awareness of my heritage, I walked through the rusting gated entrance and instantly recognized the markers of Deutch, Berkowitz, Dretel, Baumgarten, Baumel, Billig, Yeckes, Nagler, and Silberschutz. There lay my parents and grandparents and so many of their friends and relatives, re-congregated in death. I had known them all in my childhood. They either lived near us in the Bronx or visited regularly. Except for my mother, who was born in New York, the others had all been born in Zlochev. I was the only visitor in the quiet place of Zlochev that day; the noisy Long Island Expressway and the nearby Queens College that I had attended could have been thousands of miles away. I felt at home and strangely warmed as I became reacquainted with thoughts of my ancestors under the cold gray sky of *this* Zlochev, probably reminiscent of similar days in the old Austria-Hungary town many of them knew as children. Bennie Dretel, my father's dear friend, bought me my first bicycle, just after my mother died. Sam Deutch would regularly come down the street looking for me to accompany him on his seemingly endless number of errands in his big black 1939 Dodge. There was Uncle Morris, who definitively ended every statement of opinion or fact with "period, stop" to make absolutely sure that there was no argument with his emphatic, often dogmatic, declarations, whatever their content. Aunt Esther, his wife and my father's sister, next to him, was a fastidious housekeeper and had a collection of beautiful tablecloths that Uncle Morris had joked were never used for visitors and might finally be taken out for his *shiva*! The Berkowitz family, our next-door neighbors in the Bronx, were faithful friends. Mr. Yeckes drove the only Cadillac I knew as a child, and Baumgarten, I think, was the wealthiest of them all. He lived on Fifth Avenue, and I remember him dressed in tuxedo, tails and high black hat, on the *bima*, at the front of the sanctuary of Kehilat Jeshurun Synagogue on East 85th on Rosh Hashanah – regal and proud and so far from the Zlochev they had all known and left decades ago. I had a deep well of memories as I thought about Grandma, Grandpa, my parents, and their friends. I noted the dates carved in gravestones showing the long lives of the earlier generation, the premature deaths of my mother and father. It was getting dark; the wind whipped through the lonely lanes and the temperature dropped. I was still warmed by the company of my forefathers, and I did not want to leave them, to return to the expressway and the realities of New York City. I sat on a stone bench crusted with snow, closed my eyes for a few moments, and thought about the years and the people long gone. It was getting dark. I would come back here to be comforted again by the force of ancient memories, thoughts, and feelings.

———————

The Zlochev of the Austro-Hungarian Empire of my ancestors had the misfortune to be located near Lvov, approximately 325 miles west of Kiev and southeast of Warsaw. I say misfortune because, in the path of various armies going to and from Russia, Zlochev was overrun on the way east and on the way west, for centuries. It has been part of Galicia, Poland, Austria-Hungary, the Soviet Union, and, most recently, the Ukraine, at various times since the Middle Ages. Some of those transitions were peaceful, some less so. Jews were prominent in the business and the political life of the town and region from the sixteenth century. The old synagogue of Zlochev was built in the second half of the seventeenth century and was possibly where my grandparents and great-grandparents prayed, although they more likely went to a neighborhood *shul*, more fitting to their status. Both my paternal and maternal families came from Zlochev. It was a city of ten thousand people, more than half were Jews in the early 1900s, when my maternal grandfather, Joseph Silberschutz, walked out of town one day and headed northwest to Hamburg. He left that day because he did not want to be conscripted into the Emperor Franz Josef's cavalry. He was afraid of horses, some people said. Maybe so, but, more importantly, he also had a dream, held by so many of that time, that life could be better outside the Jewish community of Zlochev; life could be better in America. Others sought ways to emigrate to Palestine. He left his fiancée, my grandmother, Frieda Baumel, and walked northwest to Hamburg with a small fabric suitcase and his painting supplies. He was going to Hamburg to get on a ship to America. Sometimes he got rides with people on their horse-drawn wagons, and at one point, he took a train for several hundred miles. Although he was learned in Torah, he made his living painting houses, indeed truly decorating houses, inside and out, and he thought he could do that and more in America. His brother, Jake, also a painter in Zlochev, accompanied him on that journey.

My grandfather came to New York just after the turn of the twentieth century and got work as a painter in Manhattan. He worked hard, lived frugally, and relished the company of other immigrants from his hometown. With my future paternal grandfather, Nachman Billig, and others, he founded the Zlochev Society, a *Landsmannschaft*, a benevolent association of people from the same place that was common at the time, to ease the way for immigrants from their towns in Europe to the New World. In some ways, it attempted to recreate some of the social milieu of the old country in America and also served to raise money to help the neediest among them, to visit the sick, bury the dead, and to share in the joys, the *simchas*, that life brings. He worked as a master painter for the Lester and Lester Company for about ten years when the last Mr. Lester died, leaving the firm in disarray. My grandfather bought the company and managed its assets. Crews were in the midst of painting a building at Columbia University. In fact, they were completing the ceiling of the office of the president, Dr. Nicholas Murray Butler. It is unclear how the relationship developed, and it is a most improbable one, looking at the histories of the two men, but somehow Joseph Silberschutz, of Zlochev, my grandfather, ended up having some discussions, maybe only about paint color, but undoubtedly about more, knowing my grandfather, with President Butler of Columbia University. The two became friends of sorts, or at least that is how the family legend goes. My grandfather ended up with the contract to paint a portion of Columbia University's buildings, mostly the faculty offices and residences, and his successful career as a painting contractor was assured. As he saved money, he began to buy real estate in the Bronx and in Yorkville, amassing a significant portfolio prior to the Depression. The Silberschutz brownstone at 508 East 89th Street in Manhattan was the family home and meeting place, the site of holiday celebrations, Sunday family dinners, and all kinds of occasions, happy and sad, from the early 1920s until my grandmother's death in 1984.

Though neighbors in Yorkville called my grandfather "the mayor of 89th Street," even that title did not convey **my** childhood image of my grandfather's heroic proportions. He seemed very tall to me, although he was approximately five feet, eight inches in height. He had a warm, kind manner and a friendly, bushy black moustache. His large, wrinkled hands were reassuring to hold on to, and his slight stoop made it seem as though he wanted to get closer to his grandchildren to hear what they had to say. His deep baritone voice is something several of the men in the family are grateful to have inherited. Best of all, he always seemed to have time to enthusiastically, somewhat urgently, take us for an ice cream cup at the corner store at York Avenue and 88th or down the street to Carl Schurz Park to see the docked fireboats ready for an emergency call, the tugboats and barges that regularly plied the East River waters, and Gracie Mansion, the house occupied by the real mayor of New York. We would run on the promenade, the John Finley Walk, play in the sandbox, or, in warm weather, wade in the shallow wading pool. He was more than tolerant; he seemed to genuinely savor those afternoons with his grandchildren. I was fortunate to be one of them. My grandmother, on her rare walks to the park with one of us, especially when we were babies, would stop to chat with Mrs. LaGuardia whose Gracie Mansion porch overlooked the walkway at the entrance to the park. My grandmother claimed that Mrs. L. admired her grandchildren and said they were the "most beautiful children in New York City." Grandma, of course, believed her and quoted her frequently, disregarding the fact that Mrs. LaGuardia was the wife of a highly successful New York City politician.

One of the most vivid and enduring childhood memories of my time at the 89th Street house was of my grandfather standing in a corner of his dining room, facing east, wrapped in a *talit*, a prayer shawl, swaying in the deep concentration of prayer for a half hour or so each morning and again, if he was home from work in time, in the late afternoon or evening, without the *talit*, as was the custom among religious *Ashkenazi* men. His devotion to the ritual was complete, and we knew not to test his ability to be distracted. It was as if he was enveloped in a special aura – for him, maybe the spirit of God – which filled us, even as children, with respect and awe. His commitment to prayer and to being "a good Jew" was matched by a likewise steadfast devotion to family, to *"Landsleute,"* and to dear friends whom he regarded as family. On his rounds to visit his rental properties in the Bronx, he often got involved in lengthy discussions with his tenants, and he always seemed willing to delay their payments of rent when they were out of work or were experiencing difficult times in their families. After all, most of them were also *Landsleute*, almost family, from Zlochev, Lvov, or places nearby.

After we moved from the third floor apartment in my grandparents' house on 89th Street to the Bronx, when I was about five, my grandfather would frequently "check up on us" during his business rounds of customers and renters. He would regularly stop by our house in his then chauffeured black Dodge. Grandma felt that in the 1940s there were too many cars on the road and that it was unsafe for him to drive on the streets of New York. She didn't think he was a good driver, especially when preoccupied with business details. So, Grandpa gave in to her wishes that he have a driver, although it certainly wasn't his style. She had the last word on many such issues in the family and was, indeed, someone who ran the family from the kitchen table. I remember being home from school with a cold or sore throat, on occasion, and being absolutely delighted that Grandpa would coincidentally visit, always bringing a half dozen Hershey chocolate bars, which were a lot bigger and better tasting then than they are now. His presence was reassuring to me and to my mother, his eldest child, who savored the time with him. I guess that is one of the reasons he came by.

After he left, my mother sometimes told me stories about the old days with Grandpa, her blue-gray eyes always gleaming with pride. She told me that when she was eighteen, after she graduated from high school, in 1925, Grandpa took her to Europe to visit Zlochev. He was going not only to visit family and friends who had not immigrated to the New World or to Palestine but to bring money collected by various fundraising drives of the Zlochev

Society in New York over the previous few years. With tears welling up in her eyes, she recalled the thrill of leaving the New York harbor with the steam ship's blaring horns and smoke beginning to rise from the stacks, everyone waving good-bye to everyone else, just like you see in the old movies. I think she left out most of the seasick stuff. She noted that Grandma, true to form, had stuffed several old square egg boxes, with the dividers removed, with two kinds of *kichel*, sponge cake and honey cake, just as she did whenever we visited at 89th Street and returned home to the Bronx. Mommy felt proud to be picked to go to see "the old country" and the town where generations of Silberschutzs and Baumels had lived and died. On the first day of their visit, a "holiday" was declared and all the Jewish Zlochevites came to welcome them. She also remembered that she lent a fancy white dress that she brought with her from New York to a cousin, whose wedding they attended while in Zlochev. My mother left the dress with the young woman as one of the many gifts they had brought for family from America.

She often told me that Grandma was an unusual woman and that I should never believe her when she said, "I'm just a *hausfrau*." As a girl in Zlochev, on many afternoons, when her brothers were learning Torah, and "the girls from other families were walking on the boulevard," Grandma had to stay home and learn too. Her grandfather, the *melamed*, the teacher, had said, "She has a head like a man; she shouldn't parade on the boulevard. She should learn Torah like the boys." And so, Grandma had learned and learned well. I know that whenever I was visiting at 89th Street, throughout my childhood and young adult years, she would at some point in the day, usually at lunch, ask, "Nathan, do you know what the *parsha* (Torah portion read each week in synagogue) of the week is?" I sometimes did, but in any case, Grandma would then go on with a short synopsis, and then follow with her own, sitting-around-the-kitchen-table commentary of the portion of the Torah that had been read or was going to be read that *Shabbos* in the synagogue. She made Abraham, Isaac, Jacob, Joseph, Moses, others, and all their wives come alive, as if she knew them personally, even intimately. Hers were not always strictly rabbinical commentaries, but they were wise, nonetheless. She regularly included homey ideas like bemoaning Joseph's difficulties after leaving his family with the comment, "and he couldn't even send his mother a postal card." She empathized with Isaac being led to sacrifice as a young boy, horrified about what must have been going through his mind, and always commented that "it all worked out, with God's will." She had deep sorrow at Moses's loss of patience with his people, claiming that "he should have led us into Canaan." And she swelled with pride that Sarah had given birth to Isaac in late life. Grandma had a special relationship with her biblical heroes. They were like members of the family, and she tried to recreate that for me and for anyone else who would listen. Grandma also had a keen sense of family history and regaled us with stories of life in Zlochev and the relationship between the emperor and the Jews. She glowed with teenage excitement when she described the day that her mother asked her to sweep and wash the front steps of their house because the Emperor Franz Josef was coming to visit the town and might pass by on their street. Her mother, and she, wanted to be sure that the emperor had a good impression of the Jews of Zlochev. Something I didn't learn until after her death was that Grandma, who went to a Polish public school, could recite parts of Shakespeare's *Romeo and Juliet* in Polish.

My grandfather died in his early eighties after a fall, hip fracture, and subsequent pneumonia, in 1963. Grandma lived for twenty additional years and died at approximately 103 years of age. I say approximately because Grandma was never one to disclose her exact age. She said only that she was born on *Tu B'shvat*, the Jewish Arbor Day. She knew the *parsha* of the *Torah* that was read in synagogue every week, and much more, until well into her nineties. Grandma died on the morning of the first *Seder* of Passover, the thirty-fifth anniversary of my mother's death, at almost the same time of day as had my mother. She never got over the sadness of my mother's death, her eldest child, at age forty-two, and after her death did not henceforth refer to her by her given name, Anna. Instead, she called her, in Yiddish, *di andere* (the other one). Knowing my grandmother, it could not have been a coincidence that she died on the same day of the Jewish calendar as my mother, when at 103, any day was available to her.

My maternal grandparents were both powerful forces in my life, showing by example how to take care of themselves and their responsibilities, always trying to live caring, righteous lives, in the largest sense of the terms. They were devoted to each other, the family they loved, their rich histories, and the friendships they nurtured. Their lives set a standard, impossible to live up to, that we, their descendants, can only aspire to emulate. Whenever I am near East 89th Street, I still walk past 508, the front of which looks exactly as I remember it from when I was four or five, and later, of course. I wonder about the lives of those who now live there, but, more importantly, I still can visualize our family and all that we lived inside. That was our family home for more than half a century.

4.

MRS. GOLD

Mrs. Gold was one of my first patients in private practice and, indeed, one of my most memorable. When she initially called my office, she said slowly, in a halting and sad voice, that she was a seventy-eight-year-old widow who needed an appointment as soon as possible. She added, "By way of credentials, if I need any to get into your practice, I was a social worker in the Jewish Child Guidance Clinic a thousand years ago."

I said that no credentials were necessary and that I would be happy to see her in a few days, unless she thought that her situation was more urgent. On the phone, she had sounded intelligent and sophisticated, with a touch of New York sarcasm, but her speech was tired, slowed, possibly slurred, like a phonograph record playing at the wrong speed.

When I first saw her, three days later, it was one of those frenetic days in which I had to run from the hospital to the office and then to teach a class, so it required a quick transition to being attentive to a new patient who was going to be in significant distress. Preoccupied and still a bit distracted, I absent-mindedly barged into my own waiting room from the building corridor and almost stumbled into a frail, elderly woman who was slowly pacing around the small, carpeted space. She had short gray-white hair, which appeared a bit unkempt and in need of shampoo and brushing. Her hazel eyes were sad and sunken. Her skin was dry and wrinkled. She wore a shabby brown cloth coat which was stained along the line of buttons, as if from dripped coffee or soup, and she carried a worn paper Bloomingdales' shopping bag. It did not initially dawn on me that this was my first patient of the day. My first thought was that she might be a disheveled, disoriented woman who had wandered in from the street, past the usually vigilant building doorman.

"May I help you?" I asked.

"I'm Sylvia Gold; I'm here to see Dr. B. at 9:30," she said cautiously and with a slight lisp.

"I'm Dr. Billig. I will be with you in a few minutes. Please have a seat," I said, pointing to the chair nearby and thinking that if her appearance and grooming were indications, this old woman may be in considerably more distress than I would have predicted from our earlier brief telephone conversation. Because I would have to leave quickly after this session to get to a class I was teaching uptown, I wondered about calling Lenox Hill immediately just to check if there was an available bed in case I thought that hospitalization was necessary for her at the end of the session. I decided to wait; maybe I was overreacting. I could make those arrangements later, if needed, and even drive her to the hospital on the way to my class, if she were really in a very fragile or risky state.

Five minutes later, I invited Mrs. Gold into my office. She arrived at the center of the room and surveyed it briefly, very slowly walking around in a circle, in a kind of strange, bewildered way, seeming to be checking out this new environment, much as she appeared to be doing earlier in the waiting room. She later told me that she was very affected by "the ambiance, the feel and décor" of spaces she occupied. She said, "Since I've already determined that I liked the sound of your voice on your answering machine recording, I was just making sure that the atmosphere would be comfortable before sitting down and making a real commitment. I assume that I'll be spending a lot of time here."

There was a sweet honesty in that explanation, and I was heartened that she had the energy to go through what sounded like her usual process of assessing her surroundings so thoroughly. I was interested in what attracted patients to a given psychiatrist and certainly was pleased that my voice and décor were passing Mrs. Gold's test. She unbuttoned her coat, revealing a well-worn but clean simple cotton dress, like the "house dresses" my mother and grandmother would wear at home but never outside the house. Mrs. Gold finally eased herself down into the chair across from mine, and in a soft, sad and frail voice, with many sighs, began to tell me her story.

She had just returned to New York after thirteen months in Florida, where she "had a wonderful time with an old friend who had just died." As she spoke those words, she began to sob, quite imperceptibly, as if she had a lot to sob about but had already done a great deal of it and had little energy and insufficient tears left to do too much more right now. She collected herself a bit and said to me, with a remnant of humor, "Let me go back to ancient history."

Mrs. Gold had been married for twenty-two years when her husband died, approximately twenty years earlier. She had had a good marriage. "Sam was some man," and she missed him, but she had not allowed herself to cry much after his death. "He left me financially OK," she said, "but I had two kids to raise, and I had to devote myself to that task without stopping to mourn." She thought she had done child-rearing well, "and at seventy-eight I haven't stopped worrying about them, even though they are fully adults." She did miss Sam, even twenty years later, and daily thought of him and the good times in their life together.

A little over a year ago, she visited her friend, Gladys, on the west coast of Florida. She had looked forward to time in the sun with her old friend, with whom she had worked decades ago and kept in touch inconsistently. One morning, while walking on the beach, delighting in the sunny weather and light breeze, she and Gladys were so occupied with shell collecting that Mrs. Gold nearly walked into a tall thin, tanned, somewhat withered elderly man. He had a warm smile and a shock of wavy but thinning white hair. He had piercing "baby blue" eyes that were oddly familiar and instantly tantalizing to her, even at seventy-eight.

"Sexy, very sexy," she thought. Gladys knew him slightly from having seen him on the beach and at some "old folks" get-togethers. She introduced Sylvia to Bernie Wolfe.

"Oh my God, Bernie, of course I know Bernie," Mrs. Gold exclaimed exuberantly, without hesitation, as soon as the words of introduction were out of her friend's mouth. "We were childhood sweethearts in Brooklyn!" she whooped in a rather uninhibited outburst, which, she later thought, "might have caused an old man to have a heart attack right on the spot."

"Oh my God, this is incredible!" she shouted. The moment seemed unreal to all present, something out of a Hollywood film of yesteryear. Decades of history flashed quickly through her mind as she stared at this old Bernie Wolfe. The same must have been happening to him, but he just looked at her intently, with a slight smile. She did not know whether to embrace him passionately, which was her first impulse, or to shake his hand. They compromised with a long and tender hug as they both smiled broadly in equal, but quiet, disbelief.

With a frail but obviously joyful deep voice, trying to be lighthearted, he said, "I remember the many times your mother kicked me off your front porch; it's got to be at least sixty years ago." She countered romantically, "I remember that and so much more. You were my first real boyfriend, my first lover." Gladys realized that she was quickly becoming superfluous as she observed the incredible, serendipitous, and poignant chance meeting of two teenage lovers, more than half of a century later. She excused herself after a few minutes and later told Sylvia that she was aware that she had witnessed a rare moment in the lives of those two people. "I'll see you back at the condo, whenever I get there," Sylvia managed to say, still stunned by what had just happened.

Sylvia and Bernie began to reminisce at lunch that day at a small nearby beach café. They started with sixth grade and gradually worked their way through high school – the notes passed in classes, the school dances, doing homework together, the stolen kisses, the hours spent lazily walking in the park, the petting on her front porch and elsewhere, everywhere, and the first clumsy real sex together. She had gone to college, Brooklyn College, a year before him; he had to earn some additional money before he could go. He wanted to be a surgeon; she wanted to be a nurse or a social worker. Bernie got a full scholarship to attend Harvard just before he was to start college in New York, and "he couldn't turn it down." From humble roots, he "might have a chance to really make it in life if he went to Harvard," he and his parents had thought. They talked frequently on the telephone that first year that he went away, but their relationship suffered with the distance. Sylvia's mother was heartsick. Although she had kicked him off the porch many times, she always loved Bernie like a son and wanted him to be part of her family someday. She had counted on it. By the end of a several hours lunch that day on the beach, each admitted to the other, "I never stopped loving you," and they held each other tenderly and cried for what could have been all those many years and for the coincidence of the events that now brought them together at this very late point in their lives.

"What about your wife?" Sylvia finally asked Bernie, with trepidation, noting a gold band on his finger.

"Alice had a stroke twelve years ago and she recognizes no one. She's in a nursing home near here; I visit her every other day," he answered somberly. "And what about your husband?"

"He was a good man; He died twenty years ago; I've been alone for a long time," she said sadly.

They talked about her two daughters and the fact that he had no children. "I always wanted *you* to have my child," he said sadly.

"I almost did," she admitted with a wry smile, referring to the miscarriage she had in her freshman year at college. He had forgotten but became teary with the reminder.

By the end of lunch, he invited her to move into his condominium on the beach, after her planned week's visit with Gladys. It seemed perfectly natural for them to consider it, even on their first date in over sixty years.

Sylvia had to return to New York to take care of some personal business but promised to hurry back to him. Then they virtually lived together for a little more than a year, an extraordinary year. They continued to get to know each other again and, at the same time, to live as if the intervening sixty years had never occurred. He made no secret of the fact that he was quite ill with heart disease and "could go at any time." That saddened her but did not deter her from renewing and reviving their bond and allowing her love for him to grow without restraint. Whereas her relationship with Sam had been steady and sure, with Bernie it was passionate, at sixteen and then again at seventy-eight. Amazingly, the character of their connection had not changed over sixty years. They spent hours roaming the beach, endlessly reminiscing about family and friends, holding hands and joking playfully like two adolescents in love for the first time. If they walked too fast, he would become short of breath, even get a "twinge" in his chest and occasionally pop a nitroglycerine tablet into his mouth. He needed a daily nap in order to stay awake past eight in the evening. She reveled in his lively, sometimes sarcastic, sense of humor, his intellect, and worldliness. They discussed books, movies, and plays of earlier decades and ones that they now enjoyed together. They went to concerts and readings at the local library. They read love poems to each other while resting on the couch. They massaged each other with fragrant oil. He liked his back rubbed with sesame and she always asked for a reciprocal foot massage with almond. This was a much-delayed honeymoon – one she never had imagined. She could and did forget that their time was limited, even though the ten pills he took each day should have reminded her of his fragility. He sometimes joked, "It's amazing that each of these little pills knows exactly where to go in my body. It's magic."

"His beautiful, sexy eyes twinkled," she remembered, "the same blue eyes I fell for when I was just a kid." She felt strong and competent and well-nurtured by his presence, by his love for her. She realized that she had missed those feelings for many years.

Bernie was a retired neurosurgeon and loved to talk about his years of work – his great successes, life-saving surgeries, and some failures. He was also an expert gardener, an avid cook, and a perpetual liberal voice for all kinds of causes. He had opposed the US involvement in the war in Vietnam, wrote letters on the subject to the editor of the *New York Times*, and yearned to go to the marches in Washington but did not want to leave his wife. He was proud of his long relationship with Dr. Benjamin Spock, to whom he bore not only some physical resemblance but also similar spirit and political views. He spoke admiringly of his friend, Jonas Salk, who he said, "saved a generation and more." He felt privileged to have been a part of the medical profession with them, although he minimized his own individual contributions. "I was just an everyday brain surgeon; I did OK. *They* were giants," he would say.

One rainy day, Mrs. Gold awakened at her usual 6:00 a.m., went into the kitchen, and made their morning coffee. She returned to their quiet bedroom to find him dead in bed. Despite their ages and the many talks about his fragility and his daily diet of assorted pills, it was as if she had no warning. It was as if he was just eighteen, healthy, and strong. It was as if he had just done fifty push-ups on her front porch in a contest with one of their other high school buddies. They had fallen asleep in each other's arms just ten hours before she found him that morning; she was glad for that. He had grinned that satisfied little-boy grin of his and fell off to sleep. She had had a year like no other time in her life, but she wanted much more time with him. It was over.

Sylvia Gold went through the motions of planning what was supposed to be the simple funeral and burial that Bernie had requested. The emotional memorial service, orchestrated by her and some of his nieces and nephews, was attended by hundreds, maybe even a thousand people. The words said in the eulogies were grand, but they could not convey the joys she had felt during that year and the great grief she now suffered. Those feelings were both beyond words. They were private and she wanted to keep them to herself. Besides, no one else would understand, she thought. As she was boarding the plane back to New York, a week after Bernie's funeral, a flight attendant looked at her and asked if anything was wrong. "A friend of mine died last week," she said, with gross understatement.

I could not stop Sylvia Gold in the middle of her narrative in that first session in my office. I did not really want to. Without my being fully aware, she had talked, with a few guiding questions and comments from me, for an hour and a quarter. I was mesmerized and touched as by no other story in my young career, indeed my life. Obviously, the poignant elements of loss she described and the manner in which she described them evoked some of my own sadness. I could keep them separate from the losses in my life, I thought, but I was aware of being choked up with her story. It was an amazing life story in so many ways. Mrs. Gold was worn out by the session and her lips were parched despite two trips to the bathroom for cups of water. At the end of it, she wanted to go home, and she assured me she could manage until the next visit. She also assured me that she had no intention of "joining" Bernie anytime soon, so I shouldn't worry about suicide, "of the active or passive varieties." Over the next weeks, I saw Mrs. Gold two or three times per week. She detailed more of her history, weaving stories of her family life in New York, the years with Sam, and more about the last year with Bernie. She repeated the telling of many of the most tender moments. Her grief remained profound, and she reported that she did little except sit in her apartment for which she minimally cared. She assured me that she was "eating and drinking enough to survive." She rarely socialized, and then only with family. Since her return from Florida, she had attended no events at Carnegie Hall or the City Center, two of her favorite haunts. She wanted to "talk it all out," and before I even mentioned it, she refused to consider antidepressant medications, "at least for a few months." I agreed, because she was so involved in mourning, in talking, and seemed to be taking increasingly better care of herself as the weeks went on.

It was apparent to me that Bernie's death, while a recent and substantial loss to her, reignited the grief that she barely allowed herself to feel after Sam's death, more than twenty years earlier, and both of those re-emphasized the loss of potential she was beginning to feel in old age. Mrs. Gold had also suffered a serious postpartum depression after the birth of her older daughter. That episode she had barely acknowledged, but now that also rose to the surface for reexamination and complicated her present state.

I was concerned that her bereavement could well become a significant depression, with all the disability and risk inherent in that diagnosis. She readily accepted the notion that her current state was the result of a compilation of losses, possibly starting in childhood, but certainly in adolescence, punctuated by the original loss of Bernie early in college, then Sam's death, and then, most recently, Bernie, again. The recent trauma had reactivated old ones, but she now had fewer resources and distractions than when she was younger and felt the gratification of being a mother, social worker, and homemaker. She was still obviously a person of great substance, with many interests, close relationships, and both knowledge and interest in the arts, history, and politics. Despite several major upheavals in the past, she had mostly functioned well in her various roles and savored the positive aspects of her life. In the initial therapy sessions, she loved to talk, to tell stories of her many relationships and the numerous experiences of her lifetime. She spoke with pride of her successes, particularly related to being a wife, mother, political activist, and social worker. She cried increasingly easily over the losses. She was mourning in the most profound way I had ever seen anyone do so. Her entire being seemed bathed in sadness, and now, for the first time in her life, she was able to fully admit it to herself and share them all with someone else. I was aware that I would have to monitor and guide her carefully over the next months. She was, indeed, very vulnerable, as she gave up some of her lifelong defenses against so much sadness.

———

Over the next months, Mrs. Gold continued to have an enormous capacity for mourning, as if Bernie's death had given her the first opportunity she had ever had for such a state. Ironically, after the early sessions in my office, she reminisced more about her deceased husband, Sam, and her life with him than she did about the more proximate cause of her sadness. I supported her need to talk about Sam and their lives together. She talked about the mutual respect they shared, the children they bore and began to raise together, the mostly good times they enjoyed, and the several crises they weathered. She talked about the weekend car rides to the Catskills and the longer vacation excursions to the Adirondacks. "It seemed as though we were always striving for the peaks; we loved the mountains," she said with one of the first twinkles I had seen in her brightening eyes in six months of treatment.

"I realize that I miss him terribly, even after twenty-plus years, and I've never given myself permission to feel that fully. All these years, I was protecting the kids, now in their forties, and myself, from the horrible loss and sadness. On Sunday mornings, he would usually get up early, dress the kids, and go out for bagels and lox, which he brought back with the *Times*. That was the one day I could stay in bed, sleeping or reading, until they returned with breakfast. No matter how many Sundays passed, over many years, the kids loved their special weekly errands with their father. It was an important family ritual for all of us. There were others. Although we did not go to synagogue, I tried to at least make Friday nights special. I lit the *Shabbat* candles, and we said the *kiddush* over wine; they were some of the few religious rituals that bound us together. Those go back to both of our families, and much before that, I guess. I should have continued those after his death, but somehow, they got lost. I did not have the energy to continue those rituals without Sam. They had become too strongly associated with him, and they would remind me constantly of his absence, as if that did not happen anyway. I did different things with the kids as they got older, like taking them to movies and to shows. They loved those too. Now it is over. What am I talking about? It has been over for more than two decades. I wish I had taken better care of *myself* during those years after Sam's death. I thought I had escaped by focusing totally on the kids and my job as a social worker in the adoption section of a Jewish social service agency."

I commented, "It's been over for a long time, but until recently you've not been able to acknowledge that very much. On the other hand, part of it will never be over because you have such rich memories and associations to those years with Sam and the kids, when they were young. You have deprived yourself of thinking about them to protect yourself from the sadness. But over the years, you have also developed new and different relationships with your children, especially now that they are adults and have children of their own." "That is true, and Sam died so long ago, when the children were still young, that none of my more recent history with the kids are associated with him. That is sad too, because he would have liked the kids as adults. They would have had good intellectual sparring matches and warm embraces, and he would have gotten down on the floor and played with blocks with their little ones. He would have loved to take his grandchildren to the Bronx Zoo and to Central Park. He would have made pilgrimages to FAO Schwarz and gotten them a special toy or stuffed animal, even though he would have complained that they were outrageously expensive." Mrs. Gold became teary as she talked about what she, Sam, the children, and now the grandchildren had missed together.

"And Bernie," she continued, "he was a miracle, a flash in the heavens, like a meteor, the way he appeared, after having been such a presence in my earlier life. His intensity, our intensity, the way he disappeared a lifetime ago, and the way he reappeared again last year, only to disappear again, this time for good – those times were utterly amazing to experience. Bernie was a dividend of passion, of love that most people never get in life. I was lucky, but I pay for that luck now with exquisite pain, which I mostly keep to myself. I tell only you all the particulars. Sam used to say in his thick New York accent, 'Nothing is for free in life.' I used to argue with him about that pessimistic or fatalistic view, but, as usual, he was right."

It was seven months since Bernie's death. Mrs. Gold had resumed seeing a few friends, having tea in her apartment or theirs, but only with those who knew about Bernie's death and who could tolerate seeing her get teary looking at her photographs taken during the "miracle" year with him and the already tattered laudatory news clippings from the time of his death, which she pored over repetitively. She did not talk much with them about the details of the year with Bernie; she shared the photos and clippings. She had begun going to lunch occasionally at her favorite neighborhood Chinese restaurants with one or two people. She prided herself in knowing which two or three places in the City had the best hot and sour soup, a favorite of hers. She then also made sure that I knew their names and where they were located.

One of her two sisters, two years her senior, lived on the East Side. "We weren't really close once we got away from home; it's too bad that our lives had just gone in different paths. We saw each other a few times a year and spoke every few weeks. Since Bernie's death, Martha has called daily. She wants to be closer to me. We have had some good talks; mostly I have talked, and she's listened. Maybe that's true of everyone I'm involved with lately. As a matter of fact, Martha's the one who has gotten me back to Chinese food again. It is strange; I had forgotten how much I used to enjoy it with Sam, before we had children and when they were little. Until a few weeks ago, I had not been in a Chinese restaurant in twenty years or more. That is an unexpected fringe benefit of this mourning! Bernie didn't eat Chinese food because he found it too salty, and besides, he said he had a "kosher stomach," a remnant of the days when he lived at home and his family didn't eat pork or shellfish."

I commented on how intertwined the memories and the mourning of those two significant men in her life had become, and she responded, "Maybe one of the things that Bernie did for me was to allow me to revisit not only my passionately idealized relationship with him but also the wonderfully loving one with Sam. That is ironic. In a way, I am incredibly lucky.

"I must tell you, doctor, that I'm not doing that well. I can talk about the best hot and sour soups and the best raisin challahs in the City; that is easy for me. I am still pretty good at doing some covering up, except I shouldn't do it in here. By the way, I picked up two challahs today on the way over here, and I'm leaving one for you; it's good, although not one of the best. One day I'll bring you one of the best."

I thanked her for the challah and asked what she meant by "not doing that well."

"I always have tears in my eyes or on my cheeks or both. I still have not been to the City Center; I haven't even thought to give my season tickets away to friends. I don't sleep much. I am afraid of my reliance on Benadryl for the little sleep I do get. I've lost another five pounds in the last two months. I don't keep up with the news. I have not even subscribed to the *Times* again since I am back. I really do not do much except look at old family pictures and Bernie's clippings, which are disintegrating from all the handling. I feel old, something I have never felt, and I want to get back to myself, even though I'll never be the same person I was a year and a half ago."

"You may have the tears on your cheeks and in your eyes for a long time; that's OK. You are, in fact, doing some things that were impossible for you just a few months ago. You have high expectations for the speed of this recovery, and I understand your frustration with your feeling that you are not making progress toward getting back to the life you used to enjoy. And your lack of sleep is very disabling. We must keep in mind that you are doing the painful work of mourning the loss of at least two significant people in your life and covering a lot of history that you have largely put aside. That is a big job."

"So, I guess you should give me something that will help me sleep better and ease the sadness or depression or whatever it is. I have been holding out. It is time, already. And then I can really tell you some stories."

I agreed that an antidepressant might help her with some of her symptoms. I also recommended that she schedule a walk in the neighborhood every day, starting with just going around the block and then building up to twenty-to-thirty minutes. I thought that she minimized the extent to which her crying and reminiscing, the awareness that she was mourning two losses, her beginning to socialize, and the passage of time had helped her to better deal with her life recently. In fact, she did look and sound more robust in my office than in the initial months, when I was occasionally concerned about whether she needed to be in the hospital. She certainly appeared less disheveled. Her impatience now with her lack of resumption of activities and interests and her occasional enthusiastic expressions about Chinese food, challah, and other things were new and hopeful signs, I thought. I prescribed a small dose of nortriptyline, which was an effective antidepressant, sometimes with some sedative qualities, so that an additional medication for sleep might be unnecessary. She could continue the Benadryl at night, as needed, for insomnia. Mrs. Gold took the prescription, stood to leave, put the challah on my desk, gave me a polite but warm handshake, and showed a slight smile. The smile was new. Maybe now her progress would be more substantial. She was gradually ready to move on, I thought.

———

Mrs. Gold did not change remarkably during the first three months after the initiation of antidepressant medication. By her report, she continued to have less energy than she did a year earlier and complained that her interest and pleasure in her usual activities were only slightly increased. She seemed to be stuck in a chronic state of grief which, while no longer severe, was nonetheless pervasive and indolent. She began to dwell on her chronic physical symptoms, with more vigor than even in the first months after Bernie's death, and had taken to frequenting various medical specialists for complaints such as headaches, vague gastrointestinal upsets, and increased arthritic pain. She admitted that this behavior was out of character for her, because until now she thought of herself as rather stoical, concerning bodily symptoms, usually writing them off as just secondary to old age. She summed up her status with, "I seem to now accept widowhood as a disabled state of life. I feel as though I have shifted my great sadness from my brain into my body. That is not so good, and I don't know how to change it. I should be more over it by now."

"I think you are still grieving and it's complicated by depression, which is only partially responding to psychotherapy and the medication you are taking," I said. "It is not uncommon for some people to shift from grief into physical symptoms. Even though many people and many cultures use the one-year mark as a general time for the end of mourning, there's no timetable for grief, and after multiple, significant losses like the ones you've suffered, some feelings of grief may go on for years, and to some extent, even for a lifetime. If we decide that your day-to-day functioning is not improving, we might consider increasing your dose of medication or changing to another one."

"Somehow, I can't get used to the idea that medication fixes this problem, like taking two aspirins for a headache," she countered. "It seems so much bigger than something you just take some pills for. Maybe I'm old-fashioned in that regard."

"It is much bigger and much more painful than most headaches," I told her, "You have done a great deal of mourning and reminiscing over the past year and that, together with the medication you are taking, has helped you to function somewhat better. You sound worried that this is the best you can do and that in the years ahead, you'll be chronically sad and not like the Sylvia you remember being not so long ago."

"That's exactly right. I want the energy, the enthusiasm, the motivation to do new things, the gusto to get on an airplane and visit my kids and grandchildren, the vigor to do the political stuff and to argue, with fervor and indignation, when I hear people talk who have all the wrong ideas about things. Just a year or two ago, I was a different person." She said all of this with a full, even forceful, voice and with a zest that I had not seen her exhibit. I thought it belied her state of chronic disability, and I could appreciate what she must have been like prior to Bernie's death. But it was just a quick glimpse of that other Sylvia.

"I sometimes think that maybe I've lived long enough," she continued. I have buried two good men and raised two competent and nice children, who have in turn raised two more each. I have traveled to many interesting places, experienced a lot, and eaten foods in all parts of the world, and with all kinds of insects crawling around in some of those places, I might add. I have had great loves and lovers. I want to quit while I am ahead. I don't have Alzheimer's disease or cancer, and my arthritis is not crippling; I still can drive my car in this crazy city, even out to Shea's. You know that I used to be a rabid *Mets* fan? I would like to be like a baseball player quitting while he is still batting .300 or even .285, and not waiting until he has those lousy .200 or .220 seasons. I am not going to kill myself, but I would not mind being dead. There is some difference there, you know. On the other hand, maybe I can just muddle through and see what happens. My kids still need me around to set them straight, occasionally, on a few things. They still call me to ask my advice about things they should know how to handle, like how to deal with a situation with one of their kids – breaking curfew, not doing homework, etc. They forget that I am old and far from child-rearing, or maybe they think I still have some good intuition. But everything is so much more difficult when you are eighty. Don't get old. But I don't want you to die young either. That's a dilemma I've set up for you now!"

"Everything has been so much more difficult for you in the last year, but I don't think that it has to do with being eighty rather than seventy-nine," I said. "When you were talking a bit earlier about the energy and enthusiasm you miss, I got a glimpse of a different Sylvia. Those qualities are still a part of you and they are re-emerging slowly, of course too slowly for you. You may be having some difficulty appreciating that part of yourself, not because you are moribund but rather because you are still recovering. Recuperations of all kinds can be more difficult when you are older than when you are younger. And furthering your baseball analogy, I would say that you are in a bad slump, rather than ready to hang up your cleats."

Sylvia smiled one of her knowing, slightly condescending smiles. "It is great to have a young, optimistic doctor. I can almost believe your hopeful-ness. I do feel better after these visits; it's like taking an extra one of those little pills you give me. If you are right about my slump, maybe I should change my batting stance. That is one of the things they do in the majors, isn't it? What do you think of my making a list every night of what I am going to do and whom I'm going to see or call on the phone the next day, and then push myself to do those things to break the habit of being so damn lame?"

"That sounds like a very good idea. You might start with a short list and build up as you feel better. Including a walk around the neighborhood on every day's program would be helpful to you as well." (I had suggested the lists, walks, phone calls, and activities several months earlier, but she had ignored them then, and maybe even forgotten them until now, when she felt somewhat better; now she thought they were her ideas!). "Would you also consider joining a therapy group of people dealing with similar issues?"

"How come you didn't direct me to do the walking until now?" she asked, sounding a bit imperious and annoyed, as if I had shortchanged her. "And 'no' to the group; I want you to myself and don't want to hear other people's sad stories. I would like to see you more frequently, maybe twice per week again? I think that would help."

"Until now you have been reluctant to have more frequent visits. Let's try that; it's a good idea. And I think that I have mentioned the value of your trying to resume activities, walks and visits with people you might enjoy, but until now you have dismissed those; maybe you weren't ready. You didn't have the energy or motivation. Now, you came to it yourself because you have been feeling slightly, maybe imperceptibly to you, better, with each week, and maybe you now can occasionally feel some elements of the old Sylvia that you have not known much in the last year. You are understandably tired of being depressed, but you wonder whether you can be otherwise, after all you have been through. All of these are worth trying and I think it will be helpful. I would also like to slightly increase the dose of the medicine you have been taking and see you here twice per week."

"OK, coach. But stop saying 'the old Sylvia.'"

Sylvia Gold gradually felt better, although she did not return to her baseline functioning of the time prior to Bernie's death. Earlier in her life, she had been able to accommodate to losses she suffered, with a mixture of resilience and useful personality defenses, which allowed her to generally function at a consistently high level. Bernie's death, and what it uncovered from the past, was a severe blow to her. Coming in her later years, it challenged her usual coping abilities. Over two years, with treatment, including psychotherapy and antidepressant medication, she did return to a good level of functioning, but the scars of several old losses had resurfaced and were evident to her in her daily thoughts and activities. She did engage more easily with people, enjoyed much of her daily life, and had a somewhat more optimistic view, although a low level of sadness which she had not felt prior to Bernie's death remained. As we began a third year of treatment, Mrs. Gold decided to move to California to live closer to one of her daughters. It was a well-considered plan, and her daughter was prepared to provide care for her as necessary. Mrs. Gold died at the age of eighty-eight, with significant physical decline in her last year. According to her daughter, she remained "feisty," alert, and pursued many of her interests until the last months of her life. "Her New York edge" and sense of humor were likewise intact until the end. She often reminded me of some of the women in my family – her intellect, her warmth, her sadness. She also was comfortable with me, because, although we were more than forty years apart in age, we shared some common environments and experiences. In view of these, I always had to be vigilant that we did not fall into a too familiar relationship, while trying to make the most of our therapeutic alliance.

5.

MS. BURNS

I opened the door of my consulting room and looked to the small couch in the waiting room. Sitting there was a thin young woman with long straight blonde hair, partially hiding her face, as a veil. She seemed to have melted into the upholstery, as if she wanted to make herself small, or maybe even invisible.

"Ms. Burns?" I asked as I moved into the waiting room toward the waiflike figure of the woman. She nodded, said nothing, and barely showed her somber face.

"I'll be right with you," I added, hoping to have a few moments before our appointment time, to return a telephone call.

In a soft voice, but with somewhat pressured speech, Janet Bradford Burns had articulately told me on the telephone, a week earlier, that she was a first-year associate in the large New York law firm of Collins and Cornfeld and that she had been referred to me by a senior partner there. She had volunteered that they had recently worked together on a case, and although he had complimented her on her knowledge, skill, and diligence, he was concerned by a sense of sadness he had recently noticed in her. In a kindly way, he had asked if she was unhappy and wondered if her sadness was having any effect on her and on her relationships with other lawyers and/or clients. He asked whether she was aware of a change in herself and whether she had considered "some counseling." She had taken my name and phone number from him, and although grateful for his attentiveness to her, she feared that being considered even mildly impaired, especially by one of the senior partners in the firm, could be detrimental, if not fatal, to her career there. I was happy to get the referral from Jake Carter, a well-known litigator whom I had met at a forensic psychiatry course a few months earlier. I surmised that this bright, possibly depressed, young woman lawyer would undoubtedly be a challenging and interesting addition to my growing practice.

When I invited her into my office, I was struck by her height of possibly six feet and her ethereal beauty, as she seemed to unfold upward from her seated position and glide across the waiting room into my office. I noted that as she gently moved past me, at the door to my office, she unnaturally averted her gaze. In fact, she briefly turned her head and shoulders a full ninety degrees to face the wall away from me, as if to not risk having her gaze meet mine, when we were in relatively close proximity. After she passed me, she redirected her eyes forward, in the direction of the chairs in my office. I had not previously witnessed that kind of obviously avoidant physical behavior by anyone else. She limply sat down in the designated chair, a tan leather Eames knockoff, again appearing to dissolve into the leather upholstery. On several counts, this person did not look like a budding successful young lawyer in the hard-driving litigation section of a prestigious New York law firm. I had, of course, previously known people who were remarkably successful in their work lives but incredibly ineffective, even disabled, in their personal relationships. In her body language and manner, Ms. Burns radiated a nonspecific fragility, anxiety, and sadness even before she uttered any words in my office. My thoughts went to a large, delicate, thin, frightened young bird which had possibly strayed from her flock.

I asked her to tell me why she had come for the consultation, and immediately she began to weep, telling me how wonderful Mr. Carter, the partner, had been to her. She confessed that at several inappropriate moments, she had barely controlled a desire, indeed a "near-compulsion," to touch his hand, in fact, maybe to kiss him. She also had the fantasy that he would reciprocate. Fortunately, she had restrained herself on each occasion. She felt "overwhelmed" with gratitude that he respected her as an attorney and also cared enough to notice her upset and suggest this consultation. She spoke softly but deliberately between sobs and quickly revealed herself to be bright, thoughtful, and substantially pained by whatever circumstances brought her to this appointment.

As psychiatrists, we try to listen to the patient's story, paying attention to the here-and-now substance of what the patient says, the history, and the subtext, the underlying themes that weave in and out of the patient's words. Psychoanalyst Theodor Reik called it "listening with the third ear." We want to know "why now?" We attempt to observe the nonverbal cues that accompany the words. We note the times that are relatively undefended by the patient when we might get a glimpse into what might *really* be going on in the patient's head. We listen for what slips out, in an unguarded moment, as a first comment from a patient entering the office, "the before we begin" words, the last thoughts of a session that might delay a departure, and the "by-the-ways." We follow the stream of thoughts for both content and affect. We are interested in the patient's remembered dreams and daytime musings and attempt to help interpret them considering the patient's history. And we try to be aware of our own feelings that are stimulated as we work with the patient. Sometimes these are indications of what the patient, or those with whom she has interacted, have felt.

Ms. Burns had clearly let me know in our initial telephone conversation and in the opening words of the session that Jake Carter was not only important in her real life but that he was also overvalued, at least partially representing somebody or something else from her past, real or imagined. Her burst of sobs demonstrated not only her extreme accumulated distress but also her relief at having a place and person with whom to reveal feelings and thoughts that were painful and deeply held. And then there was her averted gaze on entering my consultation room. I wondered what feeling or fear she was avoiding with that maneuver. What was the old history of discomfort connected to that behavior? Was there an impulse being thwarted?

The juxtaposition of her tall stately, elegant appearance and well-spoken presentation on the one hand and her appearance of great fragility on the other was remarkable. I noted these early clues and questions and thought about them as the session continued. I tried to understand their meanings as I listened to her story unfold, being careful not to reach premature conclusions.

I encouraged her again to tell me about herself and more about what brought her to my office at that time; she began to do so. She said, with increasing composure, that she wasn't sure what was *really* going on with her. I asked her to tell me more of her personal history, and maybe we could figure it out together. She said that intermittently, since adolescence, she had had periods of depression, anxiety, and extreme self-doubt. She had always been able to work her way through them with athletics, a busy social life, and intensive schoolwork. She tried hard to perform well in those arenas and usually was successful. In the past six months, those "defenses" were not working so well. She was sad; she had difficulty sleeping more than three hours continuously and then had trouble falling back to sleep; her appetite was decreased, and she had lost ten pounds in the past three to four months. "Nothing is fun anymore." She had no time for, or interest in, her usual diversions and friends. She worked long and hard hours at the law firm, but her concentration was "not 100 percent" and she would too often find herself daydreaming about various people in her life, usually men. She had those "bizarre" thoughts and feelings about Jake Carter. She feared that she was becoming too dependent on him for approval and wondered whether she had a crush on him. She was worried that years of "covering up and pushing away" feelings were catching up with her, but she was puzzled because everything *should* be fine now. She had recently reached so many important goals.

Ms. Burns had gone to Harvard, both for undergraduate and law school, after attending boarding school in suburban Boston. Her family was from Marblehead, Massachusetts, and her paternal grandfather and great-grandfather "talked only to Cabots and Lodges." (I guessed that meant that they were or thought themselves to be New England elite.) Her mother's family was from Middleburg, Virginia, and her maternal great-great-grandfather, a colonel in the Confederate Army, served with Lee and was a member of the Virginia legislature. Ms. Burns grew up being taught that it was "a privilege" to be a member of her family (both sides), not only because of the wealth they possessed but because of what everyone in the family called "our special heritage." She said this proudly but with a tinge of cynicism and the slightest hint of a maternal Southern accent, through a new burst of tears. She sounded as though she now only half believed this stuff, yet it had a strong emotional tug. Her mother was a DAR, and Ms. Burns believed that she was likewise entitled. Her father was a navy admiral, having distinguished himself during the wars in Korea and Vietnam, and then at the Pentagon. He was now in what was the last post of his career, in naval intelligence. Her brother, three years her junior, left Columbia College after his sophomore year to live in a commune in Oregon. Her father discounted him as an embarrassing failure, was enraged by his lack of discipline, and since the brother's departure from the East Coast for the "wilds of the Northwest," he was rarely mentioned by the admiral.

Family life had always been rather formal. The children ate separately from the parents and guests and were cared for by a series of governesses over the years. Ms. Burns usually warmed to the governesses, while her brother often chafed under their authority and the generally rigid atmosphere of the household. Mother typically napped in the late afternoon and was not to be disturbed. "Sir" and "Ma'am" were the standard ways in which the children addressed adults in their parents' orb. Mother always referred to father as "The Admiral" when she referred to him to non-family members or to the household staff. Ms. Burns wore white gloves at the many teas served in their house and shook hands with many dinner guests, always being careful to look them in the eye and say how happy she was to meet or see them. In retrospect, these salutations had a very mechanical feel to them, and Ms. Burns shivered at the memory of feeling like a "wind-up doll" on many occasions. On the other hand, maybe those teas were good training for the business/legal world in which she now found herself. Schedules were made to be followed and, until she went to boarding school in ninth grade, homework was done right after school, unless she stayed late for sports. Dinner, bath, music practice, and reading were the usual evening activities, supervised by a governess when they were young, and later on their own.

I asked about the relationships between the family members. Ms. Burns had difficulty thinking of something to say. I tried to be more concrete. "Did you, your brother, and your parents spend any informal time together – playing games, checking homework, reading, listening to music, or just chatting about the day at school or work, how you or they felt?" I asked.

"I don't think we did much of those things together, or alone, for that matter," she struggled to say, sounding as if I was asking about some very foreign concepts. "If I did those at all, it was with my governess. Also, I do not remember ever being kissed by my parents except for perfunctory good night kisses, which were the kind where your cheeks barely touch, but your lips are squeezed to one side, so they kiss out into the air and do not disturb one's makeup," she said in a strikingly childlike way.

Her eyes stared out into the distance, and she sadly said, "I've never really thought about how peculiar those kisses are, particularly as an expression of affection with people you supposedly love; I just accepted them. That is how all their close friends also kissed. Nobody's lips ever touched skin. It is certainly good for infection control, and you don't smudge your lipstick. Ah, yes, you would not want to smudge the lipstick! I wonder if my parents kissed any differently while making love. I wonder if they made love more than the two times that produced us. I guess that a lot of kids wonder about that for all sorts of reasons."

Kisses led her to talk about her last serious relationship with a man. He had also been a law student at Harvard, but he had a dramatically un-patrician history, having grown up in a poor Italian family in lower Manhattan. "I guess that's kind of cliche – rich WASPy girl from New England falls in love with poor, but smart, Italian boy from New York," she said sweetly but minimizing his importance, and hers, through stereotypes. He had worked his way through City College and had experimented with a long list of drugs, but nonetheless managed to excel in school. She figured that he fit into some quota that Harvard Law had for people who never made it to prep school and Harvard College. He mostly wore tee shirts and jeans, usually with an old tan corduroy sports jacket or an equally old and slightly tattered blue blazer, usually purchased at thrift shops in Cambridge or Somerville. He was definitely "not preppy – no blue button-downs, rep ties, or loafers." He had a seemingly carefree, gentle, soft-spoken manner that belied his determination to move up from his position in the lower class. He was so different from anyone she had known in her sheltered "rich-girl's" life environments, and she loved his spontaneity, inquisitiveness, and the warm, affectionate way he related to people, including her. She recalled the high she got the first time she ran her hands through his soft, black, tousled curly hair. They had never met Carlo, but her parents would consider him ill-bred, unkempt, and uneducated; she had hoped never to have to introduce them, unless of course they ended up married. She feared that her mother, on hearing that Carlo had attended public schools through college, might have asked if he spoke English. Her father would classify him as "not our kind." "And he definitely was not. That was one of the big reasons I was attracted to him."

During their two-year relationship in Cambridge, she had succeeded in keeping him from meeting anyone in the family. Carlo had missed her law school graduation, where he would have met too many Burnses, as they emerged from their limousines, because his grandmother had died in the week before. When Ms. Burns moved to New York, he had stayed on in Cambridge, where he had a temporary legal research job at Harvard to earn some money until he, hopefully, found a real job, hopefully in New York. She saw Carlo only intermittently now, every six weeks or so, but, depending on job opportunities, he might be moving to the City in the next six months, and then what? She thought that she loved him, "but he really is so different"; maybe that's the real attraction.

"Then there's my law professor," she continued, "thirty years my senior." "He is a brilliant man with a quick wit, easy smile, and tall, youthful body, always dressed in casual old Brooks Brothers, and he is a great lover. I began an affair with him during the summer after the tax course he taught and continued it in varying ways until I left Harvard. He took me to cozy restaurants in Cambridge and Back Bay where we would sit talking for hours and to his cluttered walnut-paneled office where we would screw for whole afternoons or evenings on the large, soft, threadbare red couch. We made love intensely; it was amazing how much better it was than with the younger men I have dated. I worried about wearing him out! He had great lips and a gentle touch. In all seasons, we would take long walks along the Charles, go to museums and galleries, and browse in his favorite bookstores. He did not mind that I was dating Carlo; he seemed to pay no attention to the existence of that relationship. I had increasing difficulty managing both relationships and Carlo won out in the last few months I was in Cambridge. I still speak to James; he visits in New York occasionally. It's still warm and wonderful, but there's no future; he's old enough to be my father."

Ms. Burns smiled for the first time, with slight embarrassment. "I guess you think that's what it's all about?" she said coyly, appearing more relaxed than earlier in the session.

"We'll see," I demurred. "Why do you think you've come to see me *now*?" I asked.

"I guess because of all these men," she began. "Isn't it true that what gets talked about first in therapy is the most important issue?" she asked somewhat impudently.

"Sometimes it is," I said, being careful not to close other options for her and still unsure who she was.

"I guess that you are Jewish. It appears most of the shrinks that I have heard of in New York are Jewish. And you look young to be dealing with a lot of heavy stuff," she noted.

"What about my being Jewish and young?" I asked. "The Jewish part is very different from my parents and the people I knew until I got to Harvard," she answered. "My mother would say that you look like you come from peasant stock, and in case you don't know, that's not a compliment."

"Are you wondering whether I can understand you and your background and deal with your distress?" I asked.

"Maybe, but maybe I also want someone like you because you're very different from my family; maybe I'll be treated better," she commented with a blushing smile. "You look a little like my brother, although he's blonde" she continued, "and Jake Carter at the law firm is Jewish, and you have a warm ethnic appeal like Carlo." I could hear the transference feelings building; eventually I would understand them better.

"My brother's a good guy. He's handsome, creative, and rebellious as hell, especially about all the military and pretentious stuff in our family. As you can imagine, there is a lot of that. He was always trying to get outside the family, to find friends and supports elsewhere. He did not feel loved at home. I was too busy trying to be good, so I didn't really watch out for him," she offered sadly. "I speak to him on the phone every few weeks. He is still trying to find himself. He was tortured by our family life; I guess he's very scarred."

Our time was up. Ms. Burns said that she felt comfortable in this first session, and she made an appointment for later in the week so we could continue to explore her history and difficulties. She had come into the office in significant distress but had talked with increasing comfort as the session continued. She revealed some interesting material as she gave a sketchy summary of her presenting problem and family description. Her parents, particularly her father, were described as more involved with themselves and their status than with the emotional well-being of the children or, in fact, anyone else. She said practically nothing about her mother. She revealed a yearning for basic caring and nurturing and possibly a tendency to sexualize those needs. On the positive side, Ms. Burns was a bright, attractive, socially adept person, who had already achieved a great deal. She worked hard to deny or minimize the unpleasant thoughts and feelings in her life. Despite her many strengths, she felt chronic psychic pain, in the form of a sadness of enormous proportions, which she had successfully defended against for a long time. She was now finding it increasingly difficult to do so. I had a feeling that she might have some horrible stories to tell. Now, on her entry into real adult life, outside the shelter of schools, where she had particularly flourished, she had become more overtly symptomatic.

In this first session, she had attempted to size me up and apparently thought that I was a concerned listener, possessing some "ethnic" appeal, which she characterized as "warm and different from her parents." That was a good way to start a therapeutic relationship, but I had a feeling that it would not last! After the initial minutes, she mostly took charge to cautiously guide the flow of her narrative. Because she had given me some evidence of fragility, and I could not judge the extent of that in this first session, I did not attempt to challenge her defenses or otherwise confront her. Rather, I supportively listened to whatever she chose to tell me and I looked forward to seeing her again.

———

She began one of several similar sessions with an agitated shouting torrent of anger, bordering on verbal abuse, which included, "You know what's wrong with me. You know it, but for some weird reason, you will not tell me, or maybe you are waiting for me to figure it out myself. You know what is wrong? I will tell *you* what's wrong. I feel that I have a hole right there," she yelled, pointing generally to her abdomen. "I have a defect that can never be filled and so I can never be a whole person. I will always have a fundamental flaw, and when the chips are down, that flaw is exposed, and you can't do anything about it. Everything I have done, including school successes, work at the law firm, relationships with lovers, dressing well, keeping in good physical shape, is to try to cover it over. It is too late for the hole to be filled in the normal way. I missed out on a child's normal development. I missed something or maybe a lot and I can never have that back, so it will never be filled, and so how can I go on? I might as well give up. Why won't you tell me?" She whined the whine of a five-year-old.

I wondered if my idea that she sounded like a five-year-old was a clue to the approximate time of origin of her distress or whether it was the result of an insult in her development even earlier in her life. Maybe her open expressions of hopelessness and rage were harbingers of progress for our work. How much would I have to endure in this process? I wondered.

Over many sessions, I repeatedly attempted to be supportive, helping her to acknowledge her distress as something that probably originated early in her life and to see the possibilities for repair, by saying things at various times, and in various combinations, like, "Your pain is obvious, and although it is difficult to fully explain its origins yet, I understand the feeling that you have an irreparable hole caused by some kind of insult. You have upsetting thoughts and feelings that you have carried around for a long time, and you have not been able to talk about or identify their roots. At some point we may understand them more clearly, but regardless, you can go on because you also have many strengths, even though, often, you feel incredibly vulnerable. Your eventual awareness that something happened to you, maybe early in your life, maybe even before you knew how to conceptualize it, may, in time, lessen the distress. We will see. You have already built a large backlog of good experiences and healthy adult relationships that will partially compensate for insults or losses you suffered. That will continue. But you are correct; it will not totally remove the feeling of the hole. Hopefully, you will find a way to mourn the loss of what the hole represents, of what you missed out on, and move on, even if the scar is occasionally painful."

I was struck by how often these themes of early life insult were occurring in my work with several patients, and a few of them used the image of having a "hole" that could not be filled. In my psychiatric training, we did not spend a great deal of time focusing on these early psychic injuries; maybe they were not so much in vogue at that time. I wondered if I somehow encouraged or overinterpreted them. More likely, I was taught by rather classical psychoanalysts and their focus then was not necessarily on early life deprivations or insults.

Ms. Burns's regressed presentation in my office most realistically characterized her persistent underlying mental state, but I was not yet sure about the roots of her difficulties, even after a year of working with her. I had some ideas, and I was willing to sit it out with her for as long as it took to better determine those, to do some ego-lending and modeling and offer supportive and some cognitive/behavioral techniques for helping her cope more successfully.

My suggestions of profound early physical and/or emotional losses in her life were too abstract or intellectual for her to hear most of the time. Sometimes, during this period, Ms. Burns ignored them and sobbed, moaned, and whined throughout the initial and middle parts of many sessions, even bleating like an injured lamb. This was in stark contrast to the sessions of just a few months earlier when she initially presented herself and her story with composure and sophistication, even grace, at times. She still, in fact, had the capacity to dress herself up and look and behave well, even elegantly, on the way into my office. But on occasion now, she seemed to pay no attention to what I said and went on with a diatribe of her injured feelings and my inadequacy as a therapist, as if it were a well-rehearsed script that probably covered up other feelings. At other times, she mulled over what I said, dismissed it, and wished she could just feel better. In some sessions, she could be pathetic and doleful to an extreme. Although she undoubtedly had been wounded in some ways as a young child, and maybe continuously for a period of time, she, nonetheless, clung to the consistently idealized, proper, and patrician descriptions of her family, not revealing much that would reflect negatively on her heritage or specific people in her privileged family and community environments. She did, on occasion, allude to the sterility, and indeed hypocrisy, of growing up in her family and her society of "rich, haughty WASPs." As she sadly talked, my thoughts went to her internal fragility and my suspicions that some horrendous stories of abuse, incest, neglect, or gross and persistent humiliation might be lurking in her past and could eventually emerge.

If a very damaging history was there, she either had repressed it or she was consciously avoiding it. I doubted the latter. Most of the time, according to her report, while she experienced "immense inner pain," she looked, sounded, and performed exceedingly well in her day-to-day life outside of my office. That was testimony to some well-developed strengths overlaid on an inherently fragile self.

As our work continued, I continued to be struck by how her mental state was reflected in the dramatically different ways she presented in my office. On the one hand, outwardly, she could be a lovely, well-spoken, immaculately groomed and dressed, successful young attorney. While she rarely smiled, her face could occasionally light up around her thin, dimpled cheeks. But she consistently expressed feelings that she could never have a normal emotional life, because of that hole inside her that she could never repair and a feeling of persistent internal agitation, sadness, and unrest that were often debilitating. She tried not to show it in public and did a rather good job of that, but she doubted every decision she had to make, whether it concerned which law school to attend, whom to date, or what flight to take to Boston. She constantly scanned her environment for cues of approval or disapproval and had exquisitely sensitive antennae for that information. She consistently avoided eye contact with me each time she entered my office and for about five minutes into each session. I came to think of that behavior as reminiscent of a timid, injured, withdrawn, or regressed child who must slowly reacquaint with an environment and the people in it and attempt to feel secure after each separation.

There were several sessions in which she appeared in frankly regressed disarray, with her long blonde hair unbrushed and in tangles and her clothes more mismatched than usual. Rather than talk about thoughts and feelings or even the current events of her life, she would dramatically strike out at me, citing my cool manner, my lack of caring, and my "ineptitude as a shrink."

She would occasionally sob, "You don't care about me, and even if you did, you can't do anything to fix what's wrong with me." In truth, I was not sure that I could help fix her, but I thought that the best I could do was to be consistently available and supportive and not be sucked in by her taunts of verbal abuse. Where opportunities presented, I clarified the contrast between her childlike feelings of being uncared for and abandoned and her adult feelings of success and worth in various aspects of her current life.

I suggested that she could use our relationship as a model of one of the few healthy ones she had experienced, one in which I did care about her and her distress and there were no repercussions to her expressions of sadness or anger. Although I said there were no repercussions, she did test my patience in those angry, whiny diatribes about my ineptitude and hers. At the end of some of those sessions, she would suddenly look at her watch, determine that it was time to go, and seeming to pull herself together, in a business-like way, say, "So, I'll see you on Thursday. Good-bye," as if she had done her work of beating up on me and herself for the session, and it was now time to move on to the next activity. She was certainly testing me and my ability to tolerate her in a regressed condition. I thought that she must have been in this position before, with a parent, no doubt. Was I now in the role of a parent that could not or would not respond to her needs? Maybe I was the parent she was attempting to provoke into neglecting, abusing, or humiliating her in some way?

After several weeks of particularly whiny and negativistic sessions in which she persistently belittled both herself and me, I was feeling unusually frustrated about my inability to help her. I began to think, quite enthusiastically, about sending her for one or more consultations to try to understand her better and to help her, and me, achieve some relief. I called a colleague who was a specialist in behavioral therapy and another, a psychopharmacologist. Each agreed to see her for a consultation, but as I thought about referring her, several things became clear. First, she would not get substantially better from a more strictly behavioral approach and second, as I reviewed the possibilities, there really were no medications that were appropriate for her. But maybe one my smart colleagues would shed some light on her situation that would help me in her treatment. I discussed the issues with a third colleague whose work in psychotherapy I respected and concluded that although I felt tortured, at times, I was already doing what made sense, in view of her presentation, in the way of treatment.

Most important, however, I realized that in the guise of getting consultations about a difficult case, maybe I was, in fact, giving up on her, rejecting her, or at least that is how she might see it, and maybe that is what I actually wished to do. Ms. Burns had undoubtedly suffered some very painful rejections, at the hands of significant people in her life, and now was she succeeding in getting me, or influencing me, to do that or the equivalent to her – a clear example of *countertransference*, Dr. Freud, I thought. I was struck, in retrospect, by the urgency of my quest for consultants for this person and how, initially, I was able to rationalize to myself their potential usefulness. But if she was inducing in me the wish to reject her, as she had experienced it earlier in her life, that countertransference event was important to recognize for our work going forward and might lead to the origins of her early insult. While her treatment presented significant questions and challenges, she was not the most difficult patient I had ever treated. I liked her and didn't *really* want to lose her as a patient. This was interesting and stimulating work, and I thought that I had a therapeutic alliance with her, although that was not always apparent.

I might have ordinarily waited for more evidence before bringing a countertransference issue to the patient's attention, but I felt some pressure to do so because I thought that without getting to the possible underlying secrets of abuse, neglect, or humiliation that Ms. Burns held within her, there would be little or no movement for a long time to come. Although I had little hard data, I was increasingly convinced by our interactions that her profound feelings of rejection and other possible insults were the serious early life issues that influenced her perceptions of herself and others. In addition, after feeling quite inadequate as her therapist for several months, I may have wanted to assure Ms. Burns that I was a smart, competent, caring psychiatrist. I also believed that I understood her well. Our alliance was honed, it felt at times, in battle, but I did not think anyone else could really do the work better. These thoughts should have been a warning to me to be even more patient.

She began a subsequent session talking about her distress that some of the other law associates in the office rarely invited her to join them for lunch. She thought it had to do with their jealousy of her relationships with some of the partners, with whom she worked closely on several recent cases. The partners did not invite her to join them either, because of the virtual law firm caste system, and she often felt alone in the firm, particularly around lunchtime, although there were some other people in the office with whom she could have had lunch. She felt the loneliness viscerally, experiencing a pain in her stomach that exaggerated her hunger. The association of rejection and feeding was another hint, verifying my idea that she had an early life insult. I commented to her that the association was worth pursuing.

She bristled past her sadness. "So, what does that do for me," she said in a surly way. I ventured forth, possibly prematurely. "Recently, I've discussed with you the idea of your seeing some consultants to try to help us better understand and treat your pain, and you certainly can still do that, but more important I have realized that my suggesting and arranging those may have been my way of rejecting you."

"I didn't feel it as a rejection. I thought you really didn't know how to help me out of this, and you were looking hither and yon for assistance," she said rather sweetly and supportively. "I think you work hard on my case."

I wondered whether I had made a mistake. I did feel enormously relieved that I had appreciated this powerful countertransference rejection idea and now felt that I could sit with her more easily even if she entirely dismissed it. I thought that, at least unconsciously, I *had* sought to reject her, just as her father or mother, or possibly both, had done at some early times in her life. I wondered again why Ms. Burns did not perceive the prospect of "sending her away" to consultants, the way I proposed to do it, as a rejection. On the contrary she said that she saw the whole consultation idea as evidence that I was doing the best I could with "her case." That reference to herself as "a case" was an interesting way to emotionally detach herself from our work together. Maybe she could not fully own up to the negative stuff yet, for fear of destroying our relationship. Was she now, in my office, defending against the painful feelings of rejection and hurt with her very mature, supportive pose, just as she had defended against insults early in her childhood by always trying to be good and proper? I continued, "I wonder if you are defending against some sad and angry feelings toward me, by trying as hard as possible to be the good, mature girl."

Tears welled in her eyes and then streamed down her cheeks. She paid no attention to them, but with an eerie grimace that briefly distorted her handsome face, she said, "How would *you* feel if your mother told you that the worst day of her life was the day she found out she was pregnant with you?" *This was the first crack in the porcelain facade of this aristocratic, very proper family,* I thought.

"And that was just the beginning," she cried out. "I don't know what happened during the pregnancy, but she sure as hell disappeared after the delivery, or so I was told. She never held me, never touched me, never smiled at me, except when she was showing me off to someone in my little starched white dress with a pink ribbon, and I had to smile and perform politely like a marionette. I obviously do not remember my earliest months or even years, but I know these things in my gut, and because people told me, later in various ways, how removed she was. And photographs of the time prove it. There were no photographs in which I was being held, kissed, or even touched by anyone. I was not a smiley child to say the least. I was dressed up, propped up for show."

This was some of what we have been working toward, I thought to myself.

"I've never told anyone how rejecting she was and how hard I worked to try to win her over. I have not yet stopped trying. And of course, one cannot speak of such things in our family. You can't ask for more of anything because you have so much; you have everything, except what you *really* need," she continued without catching a breath and with tears washing over her baby-smooth, now ruddy, cheeks.

Ms. Burns suddenly settled down and sighed deeply, with a slight shudder of her upper body. "I suspect that my mother was an alcoholic or maybe some kind of abusive pill-taker. From occasional hushed conversations in the house, I garnered small bits of information. I think she was hospitalized or otherwise sent away for most of my first year of life. She was a disgrace to her family and my father's, and that is the way they dealt with it. She was banished. My father certainly engineered it in his usual cold, calculating way. When she returned home, she was a zombie or that is how I remember seeing her at age three or so. That is my first visual memory of her. Maybe she had a lobotomy or shock treatments or was on some heavy sedatives. Gradually, she recovered her poise and social graces, but she was never interested in me, except in the most superficial ways. She always went to the mother-daughter teas with me at school or at the country club, but I thought that it was mostly so we were seen by the other mothers of her social set, not so she could spend time with me. I was happy for crumbs; I was glad she was there in whatever way she could be. I wondered many times over my childhood if she was really my mother. I had the fantasy of being a Cinderella, albeit in a golden cage." Ms. Burns sobbed at her mention of that image.

I may have handled the issues clumsily and without a clear view of what was ahead, but that session was a turning point in our work, at least for a while. Although we were only a bit closer to understanding the origins of her pain, there was now a crack in her lifelong defenses, and it was not yet catastrophic to her or to me. I came to feel that we now could really begin working together on some of the issues at the core of her problems. Much of what had preceded this session was a verification of her strong defenses and a test, by her, of my availability and caring. Although she continued to talk about "the hole" and her sometimes "excruciating," albeit nonspecific, psychic pain, and although she sometimes was very frustrated with our not finding a cure, she began to see me, more frequently, as a consistent ally. She intermittently genuinely accepted my view that she might do well enough, or even very well, by gradually establishing a new history, based on new relationships and experiences and a self-concept based on whom she was now, while still acknowledging the hopefully diminishing anguish of the old narrative of her life. Because at least some of the original insults may have occurred at a pre-verbal time of her life, all we might ever know of these old injuries is her persistent affect, enhanced by the stories and innuendoes of others. There might not be words to fully define the humiliation, abuse, or neglect that had begun in her infancy or early childhood.

———

In the session that marked the end of two years in psychotherapy, Ms. Burns entered the office with a rare bouncy step and a coquettish smile, although she nonetheless averted her gaze, as usual, as she passed me at the door. She carried the latest *New Yorker*, which had arrived with our office mail, earlier in the day; I had placed it in the waiting room, without reading it, only an hour before the session.

She began, "Did you read the article on psychoanalysis in this *New Yorker*?" Without waiting for an answer, she continued, "I'd love to have this one. I thought I would take it home with me; it is fascinating. You have them out there for people to take, don't you?"

I was taken aback. This reminded me of just one or two patients I had treated, who became upset when I discovered them retrieving their groceries from the refrigerator in our clearly private kitchen/mail room and advised them that the area was personal space for my officemate and me. One said that "it didn't even cross her mind" that the kitchen and refrigerator were private, and she protested vociferously that the perishable items she often purchased at the local gourmet shop, on the way to her psychotherapy sessions, would spoil if left unrefrigerated. "Besides, I never looked at the mail or the notes you left for your officemate in the kitchen," she said defensively.

Unfortunately, she was so incensed by my setting limits about the privacy of that room, that she was unable to work on other issues that might have been involved in her desire to use the refrigerator, including having a special status among my patients and intruding on my privacy. That patient left treatment shortly thereafter, complaining that I was "far too uptight for her needs."

"Actually, the magazines are there for people to read in the waiting room," I said to Ms. Burns, trying to clarify the reality and set a limit before we got into the underlying issue, but hoping also to not appear "too uptight" again. I was startled by her assumption that the magazines were left on the table in the waiting room for people to possibly take home, just as I was by the refrigerator encounters.

"You mean you won't let me take it? I could have just slipped it into my bag. You wouldn't have even known it had disappeared and, unless you check your magazines after each patient, you certainly wouldn't have known which one of your patients took it," she said with an increasingly indignant tone.

"But you *did* mention it to me, and I think it's important to look at that fact and at what is involved in your desire to take one of the waiting room magazines home," I said.

She continued, disregarding what I said and becoming more petulant, "I can't believe you're making such a big deal over one lousy copy of a *New Yorker*."

My first thought was to inject some humor, pointing out that she must know how important every copy of the *New Yorker* was to the waiting rooms of New York psychiatrists. I restrained myself. I tried to emphasize that the actual magazine was less important than the feelings and thoughts surrounding her desire to take it and the many issues concerning that wish. Also, the fact that she did call it to my attention must have some significance, beyond her just deciding to walk off with the magazine. I knew that she was not oblivious to the actual purpose of the magazines in the waiting room, but she did act strikingly obtuse on this subject. I had not found her obtuse on many other subjects so far.

"Wait a minute, are you or aren't you going to let me have it? If you were any kind of a *mensch* (You see, I know some of your Jewish words), you would just let me have it and then you could go up to the corner newsstand and replace it, later in the day or tomorrow, if it was so important to the smooth functioning of your office or the welfare of your other patients," she continued in a lately uncharacteristic, raised voice of mounting, entitled rage.

"No, you can't have the magazine, but your anger and other feelings stirred up over this are worth looking at," I said as calmly as I could, although I was a bit stunned by the extent of her reaction, especially since this degree of overt entitlement had not previously surfaced in our work together. *Maybe I am too uptight on these issues*, I mused to myself. *No, this is relevant to our work and it was relevant to the food-in-the-refrigerator women as well. This must have some transference meaning.*

"OK, forget it; I'll buy it at the newsstand myself, but I think that you are inhospitable and cheap. You know, some shrinks have free coffee for their patients. For what I am paying you, I should at least get an occasional magazine out of it," she continued, appearing, I thought, to be more composed than just a minute or two earlier and attempting a bit of jocularity to minimize the effect of her previous stance.

"I've been coming here for two years and little has changed," she said. "I still feel as though I'm not whole and never will be."

I wondered if my calm and reasonable limit-setting in this incident was, in fact, a relief to her, somehow in contrast to what she had experienced from authority figures earlier in her life. "So the magazine would be a special two-year present that might make you feel a bit better even though you don't feel whole?" I ventured.

"Giving me the magazine would show, in some small way, that you cared about me. It obviously would not make up for everything in my life; you and it are neither that important nor that powerful," she said pouting like a young child. "But I think you are being a bit of a prick about it. It is only a magazine, and I don't want to go into all the feelings that you think are so important. You should read the damn article yourself," she said, throwing the magazine on the table near her chair. "It might teach you something."

"I had a dream since I last saw you – last night as a matter of fact," she continued, as if the preceding episode had not occurred and clearly wanting to move on with the next order of business. Her testing me on the magazine issue was apparently over from her point of view. Or was it over? I wondered how the dream would relate to the session's opening material.

"So, in the dream I was in Yellowstone Park or some national park like that, and there was heavy traffic on the road, you know, like on the one from the Tetons to Yellowstone. Have you been there?" She did not wait for an answer. "Suddenly, all the cars ahead stopped completely, and everyone was getting out of the cars and walking ahead to see if there was an obstruction, maybe animals, on the road. As I approached near the front of the line of cars, I saw several, maybe three or four, cute little baby bear cubs playfully running on the road, and then they were running toward several big men, maybe park rangers, who were making concerted efforts to lure the little bears to them, on the side of the road. No mama bear was in sight. When the animals came close, the rangers clutched each of the cubs to their chests, as if to keep them safe from something, possibly from the traffic.""That's it! That is the dream," she said, seeming satisfied.

"So, what comes to your mind?" I asked.

"Let's see. We certainly never took family trips to the national parks, like the many families in those cars in that long line of traffic or even like many of my classmates at prep school. I am not sure I would have wanted to, anyway, considering my family. I did go to Yellowstone one summer with college friends and we had a blast. We camped out, cooked great meals on a fire, drank wine, smoked dope, sang songs, walked around the campsite topless, had sex under the stars, and saw bears, moose, buffalo, and all kinds of beautiful birds. And the geysers were amazing! I remember feeling very free, as if some tremendous burden had lifted from me. I naively wondered at the time if that was caused by a magical difference between being in the

West versus the East or the communing with nature and the woods. So, in this dream, the bears were running around, romping, but I guess they were also frightened by the cars, and the tumult of the gawking people, and maybe by the apparent absence of their mama, their parents. Then they got rescued, or at least protected, for the interim, by that group of strong men. Obviously, the rangers could not hold them forever, but for the short run, they must have been comforting." She stopped and appeared pensive.

"Any other thoughts?" I asked.

"Being in Yellowstone represents my being free of Marblehead, where I grew up, of New York, of my father's damn US Navy, Harvard, the law firm, my family, and everything I know to be constricting and inflexible and never giving or supportive. That might be an exaggeration; they are not all that bad, but the park is a metaphor for openness, natural beauty, fresh air, freedom, etc. compared to what I am used to. That time with my college friends we were all equal, no hierarchy, no ranks, no bullshit, all fun. And then the bear cubs, I really identified with them, I guess. They could be me too, romping when I have an opportunity to do so, but also frightened when I feel in potential danger in the real world or worried maybe that I had, and have, no visible parents, none that I can really depend on, for emotional things, that is. So those rangers came to the rescue. They hugged the baby bears tightly, in a kind of unusually loving way for a human and a bear to be together. Do you think those rangers are you, doctor?"

"I guess so," she added quickly but thoughtfully. "And maybe Jake Carter, at the law firm also. Funny, those rangers didn't look Jewish! And you would never hug a patient, would you? That would be as odd as a ranger hugging a bear to comfort her?"

I was still surprised whenever Ms. Burns demonstrated her ability to move, during a session, from a rather regressed state, as with the *New Yorker*, to an impressively logical, thoughtful, introspective, and even humorous position within minutes. This kind of switch had become more common in the recent sessions, as differentiated from the more pervasive primitive states that characterized many of the earlier sessions of the prior year. I agreed with her overall analysis of the dream and did not push, at the time, for more specifics or clarification of the various elements and feelings she had mentioned or alluded to. She understood a lot of its meaning. For sure, we would return to some of the issues, but it was important, I felt, for her to savor the sense of mastery she showed in carefully looking at her dream. The exercise of retrieving and retelling the dream and her associations to it was a good demonstration of Ms. Burns's beginning to work through her deep feelings of abandonment and her yearning for parental love. It also reminded her of the lack of consequences associated with expressing herself with a degree of emotional freedom, and therefore her not having to perform according to the rigid and potentially punitive family norms. I thought that the dream clearly expressed aspects of her positive transference to and identification with me as a strong, supportive, caring, and limit-setting adult (parent), which she was increasingly able to accept and even welcome. Her realization that the rangers were available to temporarily protect the cubs and show caring and support, because a "mama" was not available, was poignant.

Ms. Burns had started to succeed in attempts to find and strengthen healthy relationships with some of her law firm partners, colleagues, and new friends, who might fulfill some of her mature needs. Her movement in the session from the entitled child, hungry for the crumbs of a gift, *the New Yorker*, from a parental figure, to collaborator in the healthy process of analyzing her thoughts and feelings in and around the dream was striking. In her easy shift from the magazine episode to the dream, she demonstrated a transition from the earlier incident that was something in her old personal narrative that she still had to experience periodically and then pass through, before moving on to the more healthy adult position in the analytic process, where she could acknowledge that greater personal security was possible.

Ms. Burns was beginning to see herself more consistently as some-
one who could have good relationships, mutual respect, support,
even love from appropriate people around her. These were not

feelings that came easily, and certainly not automatically, to her. Rather, her basic assumption still occasionally existed – that even if she scanned her environment carefully, with her sensitive "antennae," and tried to fulfill every expectation of those around her, she would still likely fail, be rejected, and not get what she needed. In the process, she would feel anxious and insecure. She now, increasingly, had the tools to continue to change, very slowly, over time, building some relationships, having experiences that were affirming, and valuing herself for her many positive attributes. She was a challenging patient who required that I be steady, attentive, and caring, as well as sensitively and sensibly limit-setting. She had experienced few people like me in her life to date, and she risked some new ways of relating through our therapeutic relationship.

6.

DR. ADLER II

During the first nine months of analysis, I thought that I had wasted a considerable amount of time. Dr. Adler had come back from "vacation" and his medical treatment in apparently good shape. I dealt with my worry about his longevity, during his absence, on my own, although with our resumption of sessions, I was alert and straining to assess his mental and physical status. He seemed pretty much the same as when I had last seen him, maybe a bit thinner. Then again, psychoanalysts are far from transparent. I again felt the luxury of being there in Dr. Adler's office and felt indulged to have this man listening or pretending to listen to all my drivel. I had given him the high and low points of my life and had discussed the "why now," which I ascribed to wanting to be a psychiatrist with as much knowledge of my own psychic functioning as possible. And then there were those occasional anxieties and self-doubts, which I should understand better.

As much as I wanted to be a good patient, I thought that I was avoiding the meat of some subjects, as I had my whole life and as had other members of my family, for generations. It is exceedingly difficult to really know one's feelings in the first place, and then it is even harder to be honest about them without a lot of resistance and defensive thoughts and behaviors. In analysis, although I knew a lot of the theoretical constructs, I was regularly impressed with how just talking about the everyday activities, thoughts, daydreams, etc. led to the bigger themes about what "made me tick." Of course, it was not quite that easy.

I was often struck by the fact that those of us who survived in the family had done quite well in most aspects of our lives. We were mostly well-adjusted, educated, productive citizens with generally good relationships, marriages, and families, and those who had children had produced a group of seemingly well-adjusted, smart, good kids. When there were crises, as there are in all families, we had largely weathered them successfully. Most of us were starkly aware of the impermanence and imperfections of life, as deaths of significant people in the family, young and old, had touched us all. Many of us enjoyed getting together for small and large family events, on special occasions or just for a weekend visit. We made an effort to get together to celebrate Thanksgiving weekend every year, and thirty to forty or more of the descendants (and spouses) of my parents often attended. We supported each other during stressful times and significant losses. Many were involved in interesting careers or jobs. No one was banished or written off, and we were accepting of at least minor deviations from the norm. For better or worse, several of us had become psychotherapists of one kind or another; that may be a special kind of adaptation to a tumultuous early emotional life. Some of us had also become patients.

While I relished the idea of being a patient and was curious about "what made me tick," I abhorred the notion that I had some "symptoms," which, in part, brought me to analysis. Like some colleagues, I had hoped to be able to skirt the whole truth by saying that I was a patient in psychoanalysis because it would be helpful or necessary for me professionally. Sometimes, mental health professionals try to get by with that, and several I know revealed in one way or another that they never really dug too deeply into themselves, but they could nonetheless proudly say, to themselves and others, that they "were analyzed," as if it were a credential to put on one's *curriculum vitae*. One colleague avoided the analytic process as much as he could, with the ultimate resistance, regularly falling asleep on his analyst's couch. I am not sure what the analyst did during those sessions, but one could imagine them as two *New Yorker* cartoon characters snoring away on adjacent couches for forty-five or fifty minutes, at the usual fee, of course. I did think that for the extent of my actual symptoms, which would have been considered minimal by most people, I would not have sought treatment were I not a professional in the field, and possibly headed toward becoming an analyst myself.

I fully understood the desire to either avoid, minimize, or even sleep and partly wished at times that I had the constitution to do one of those better than I did. I could never have slept in a session: that would be such a waste of the money I was paying and not at all in keeping with my family ethic of obtaining value. Except for those rare extra morning coffees or an extended breakfast, I was too goal-oriented or too rigid to purposely waste an analytic session. I did plenty of wasting with my tendency to obsess, deny, or otherwise not confront my thoughts and feelings while lying on the couch. Realistically, I knew that I had, buried within me, some painful personal and family history to sort out, and it was already catching up with me in the form of symptoms. Because I had successfully covered up so well for so long, I regarded the presence of any symptoms as a stunning and colossal defect, almost like the stigma of having syphilis, which fortunately I did not ever have. People whom I had gotten to know socially and professionally in the years during residency training, and since, were often surprised that I was a psychiatrist because I seemed so "normal" to them, unlike most psychiatrists they knew, who were "eccentric, weird, even crazy." I felt quite normal, but I also knew that that was sometimes a bit of an act, which I was good at performing as are most people walking the streets of Manhattan. Others had little or no realization what and how much I was hiding, and I possessed only a bit more knowledge of those issues. I guessed that was true of most of my friends and colleagues; we do not wear our emotions on our shirtsleeves.

I had years of mild dread which I did not accurately label as anxiety and had earlier described as just that "pit of my stomach feeling." I had it when something did not go the way it was supposed to go or where there was a threat, real or imagined, to things not going right. In kindergarten there were the episodes, as we moved away from "circle time," in which there was sometimes a mysterious small puddle on the floor. Of course, no one ever owned up to the puddle and the teacher neither confronted nor comforted any of the students. For that matter, as far as I could tell, she never attempted to deal with the fact that some child in the class was sitting there, for part or most of the day, with stinky, wet pants. I guessed that by the time he got home his pants were mostly dry. While I had feelings of humiliation, by proxy, for whomever it was, I did not suffer any dire consequences from these episodes and was able to contain my feelings of identification with him. But I was aware of my sensitivity to the subject. I thought that it could have easily been me and it reinforced my determination to try to go pee, in the school bathroom, at least once in the morning and once in the afternoon, whether I really needed to or not.

A greater trauma of elementary school, which sounds a bit ludicrous decades later, was the fact that I did not learn to skip until I was about ten years old and I'm not sure why. I had cleverly, but anxiously, figured out various ways of avoiding parts of every elementary school gym class and recess and would spend inordinate amounts of time hiding out in the bathroom, in some corridor, or behind a post or column for what should have been enjoyable parts of the school day. Although others would not necessarily realize it, skipping turned out to be a major activity in the first few years of my childhood education, and I would get nervous whenever it loomed on the horizon. I developed a powerful awareness for the imminence of a game which included skipping and would prepare and then make my getaway. I never thought to speak to a teacher and confess my disability nor to tell my parents or siblings about it, so that I could learn how to skip. It could not be that hard! Interestingly, the teachers never gave any evidence that they observed my peculiar behavior. Maybe the inattention by the teachers in both instances was as upsetting to me as was the specific issue.

Yet another arena involved the rare occasions that my parents and all my siblings were out on a weekend evening, usually Saturday night. I always got upset about being left behind. I made a horrendous fuss, crying bitterly when I was left with a babysitter, even at age six or seven. Dr. Adler commented that my presentation of these childhood anxieties was not so remarkable in themselves, since many children don't like to be left with babysitters, etc., but what was particularly poignant were my empathic observations and the fact that all the examples involved parental figures not being available, aware, or attentive to one's needs or neediness. A theme was developing!

Following on Dr. Adler's hypothesis, my thoughts went to the times when there was a substitute teacher. Even in the later years of elementary and junior high school, I would be concerned about how long the regular teacher would be away and try to find out the reason for her absence. I would sometimes be relieved to hear that she was away only to attend a wedding or some other family occasion rather than because of an illness. None of my classmates seemed the least bit interested in why or how long the teacher might be out. They thought it was fun to have a substitute, who usually didn't have a clear idea of the academic goals of the day nor much disciplinary prowess. At summer camps, when I was ten or eleven, I would sometimes get nervous when the regular cabin counselor had his day off and the junior counselor took over, even though there were no real repercussions to the change.

I realized, even before I became a psychiatrist, that these kinds of incidents involved some real or threatened uncertainty or deprivation and/or some disappointment with or potential loss of a parental figure. Whenever I mentioned these kinds of vignettes, Dr. Adler had a "field day," as I knew he would. I was disturbed that I had this stuff inside of me and, in a childlike way, would have liked to blame the analytic process for bringing it out, or even better, for producing it. The origins of my old upsets were apparent as soon as I closed my mouth and he opened his. He came back frequently to the loss of my mother, occasionally to my father's inconsistent moods, and to my not being able to count on things turning out the way they were supposed to. The themes were so obvious, and the dysfunctional automatic responses of my narrative were unfortunately so durable.

"I wanted things to go smoothly, dammit! Wasn't I entitled to that at some point! Aren't most kids?" I shouted at the analyst one day toward the end of a session. A few minutes later, in the lobby, I shook my head at the craziness of these moments on the couch which could generate so much emotion with Dr. Adler, so many years after the real determining factors. "A healthy regression" it might be called in the analytic technical world. Dr. Adler had pointed out that it was certainly "overdetermined." (By "overde-termined" he meant that there were multiple unconscious antecedents to a feeling, thought, or symptom, stemming from experiences, relationships earlier in one's life.) I did realize that many kids have far worse problems.

Another whole set of concerns involved my status among peers. The patient before me in Dr. Adler's office on several days of the week was a fellow about my age, whom I thought I recognized as being another psychiatrist in the community but did not know. He usually carried a motorcycle helmet with him as he left his session. After a few passings in the waiting room, in one session I started with, "I cannot believe that guy, a doctor, maybe even a shrink, rides a motorcycle around this city. What is he? Suicidal?"

Dr. Adler let me go on, deriding the previous patient for his lack of judgment, his unfriendliness (he did not so much as nod at me). Although seemingly disconnected, I went on to talk about my ultra-orthodox cousins and how uncomfortable they made me feel as a child. They studied constantly and knew so much about the Torah and Talmud, and there were all the ultra-orthodox religious rules they followed that I knew much less about. We were "moderate-orthodox," by comparison, if there was such a category. For a while, as a child, one of the concrete distinctions I made between their orthodoxy and ours was that they tore sheets of toilet paper in advance of *Shabbat*, so they did not have to do that "work" on Saturday, and we did not make those preparations in advance! And then on to my older sibs and how smart and accomplished they were. "Because I was so much younger,

I guess I got a free ride in terms of performing in school and just knowing things. Everyone seemed so smart when I was a kid, and at some point, I would have to show that I was too."

Dr. Adler seemed anxious to get something down for the record, but I was talking nonstop. He summarized when I finally took a breath, "So you are worried about your status if you can't successfully compete with the patient before you in this office, your cousins, your siblings? You have to work hard to not feel like the black sheep or the afterthought. Competition was a major aspect of your family environment."

"I guess so," I confirmed perfunctorily, and then verified to Dr. Adler that, in fact, I was born seven and a half years after my brother, and I was likely an afterthought or a mistake. "But my family was also very loving, and I was mostly treated like I was special, particularly by my sisters."

Despite real data to the contrary, I would often fear that I was only barely adequate to compete with peers and would genuinely be surprised that I was, in fact, highly valued, particularly as a student and later, as a neophyte physician/psychiatrist. I expected, but was also surprised, to be offered the prestigious job of chief resident in the psychiatry department. This negative, doubting view of myself meant that during college and medical school, I expressed my views on controversial issues cautiously and only rarely volunteered to discuss a subject, ask or answer a question in an academic setting and then only when called upon or, rather, when forced against the wall. The unspoken responses in my head were always correct, even better, often, than those expressed by my more assertive classmates or colleagues. Peers, I thought, regarded me as a quiet but competent, responsible, steady, and reliable guy. And maybe I was a bit on what would now be called the "nerdy" side, or whatever the equivalent was at the time. Those corduroy pants and flannel shirts of grade school epitomized my self-concept for a long time to come. They were symbolic of my condition for many adolescent and young adult years.

I had a lot of friends and had good times with them. I always got along particularly well with my peers, both boys and girls. The girls of my own age persisted in seeing me as "cute" and "a good friend." Unfortunately, this continued somewhat through college, even though I sometimes had more romantic aspirations. I was not a particularly natural athlete, so I was always a little anxious when sports became a significant focus of time together with other boys, but I never shied away from participation after my years as a "non-skipper," and I always enjoyed the camaraderie. When we "divided up" sides for a neighborhood game, I accepted the notion of being picked *among* the last but never *the* last, for stickball, basketball, and the like, because I knew that hand-eye coordination was not my forte. During the summers, at camp, I did develop significant skills as a swimmer and canoeist, although those were not exactly everyday sports when I got back to the Bronx. Later, I did go on to teach those at summer camps.

I always thought of myself as shy as a child, adolescent, and young adult. Later in life, I had difficulty appreciating the view of others who saw me as gregarious, even charming. Those were two adjectives that were completely foreign to my self-concept, behavior, or presentation. As a result of my early analytic work, however, they rang true as ways in which I tried to endear myself to others.

I had to admit, at some point in the analytic process, that Dr. Adler was usually right. The evidence I was giving him was overwhelming. I never fully mourned my mother, and I would have loved to replace her, although my overt behavior, my defense, generally, was to be super responsible for myself and ready to take care of anyone in need around me. I tried to be in charge of myself and of every situation and relationship I encountered. More than once, Dr. Adler said in his kindly, concerned, furrowed-brow way, that truly expressed the gravity of the statement, "you weren't ready to lose her." Few people are, I have since found out, no matter how old the mother or how old her child. The first several times he said that I accepted it intellectually, and eventually I conceded; sometimes I even choked back tears as he broke through my defenses, repeating it at poignant moments. I am not sure that I will ever fully get over it or that anyone completely does, especially when losses of significant people occur early and are compounded over time. But it made it easier to "know" it about myself.

We are a family that knows painful tragedies, although we do not necessarily know what to do with the feelings they arouse. Mostly we suppress them. I suppose that no one is great at it, and it is sad to have personally become an expert on the subject, especially within one's own family. I felt that I shocked Dr. Adler, and myself, with the several losses we had endured to that point, and when I talk about it, even now, I am incredulous that we, the survivors, have been so resilient.

I had earlier told Dr. Adler that my father had committed suicide with an overdose of sleeping pills, four years after my mother's death from breast cancer, when I was twelve and a half. I had never fully focused on it or its effects on me, but I know that I was devastated when I was told the news by my brother-in-law, Stu, who picked me up at summer camp when it occurred. I felt suddenly drained of energy, deadened and pained in a way from which I thought I would never recover. Was life as I knew it over? Who would see me through the rest of my life? I was twelve and a half and orphaned. I was told initially that my father died of a heart attack, and only months later did I learn the true cause of his death from an "overdose of sleeping pills." It was a shock that scared me, and I wondered about the repercussions to our family, and specifically, to me.

How could he do that? How much pain must he have endured? I was spared some of the most painful feelings of those days, and continuously through life, because of the very protective, supportive emotional umbrella of my immediate and extended family. I surely felt that "pit of my stomach" feeling for several months, but I was quickly swept into a new life and a new environment, planned by my older siblings and my devoted aunt and uncle, Martha and Harry. After my father's death, I moved into an apartment, and then a house, with my sister, Cecile, and her husband, Stu. They were twenty-two and twenty-four at the time and had a nine-month-old son.

They became my loving, caring surrogate parents, and I lived with them for the next ten years, through high school and college, until I entered medical school. Stu was fond of saying, in one of the few Spanish phrases he knew, "*Mi casa es su casa*," and their home truly did become mine as well. Over the years following my father's death, I also spent frequent weekends and vacation time in the homes of my sister, Lois, her husband, Joel, and their children at various locations in New England. Because of the love, attention, and naturally easy acceptance by my sisters, their husbands, and my young nephews and nieces, I didn't confront some of the most dire feelings of loss, at least in the short run, and my life as an adolescent proceeded in what seemed to be a pretty normal course.

My father had had a history of serious depressions earlier in his life that I knew nothing about as a child, and he had little capacity to deal with the catastrophic loss of my mother. He also had intermittent manic episodes with excesses that I only remember as being fun for me at that time. I remember my excitement when, every Friday evening for *Shabbat* dinner, he brought home several boxes of cakes and candy from the bakery near his store, the boxes tied together with light string in a kind of tower, more than we could eat on a weekend. And I loved the ten shirts from Lord and Taylor that he bought for me one time, when I was nine years old. Clearly, I did not need so many. Regularly, he would stop at Lord and Taylor, Gimbels, or Saks and buy several dresses and blouses for each of my sisters. Many of them were later returned via the "UPS man." And there were other excesses, none of which seemed outlandish to me at the time. He was diagnosed, by a psychiatrist he consulted, with what was then called manic-depressive disorder (now, bipolar disorder), although there were no good treatments for it in the early to mid-1950s. Lithium carbonate was not on the horizon as a treatment and various anticonvulsants, now often prescribed to treat bipolar disorder, were yet to be discovered. His mood swings were never so extreme that he needed hospitalization, but his unstable mood did interfere with his life, and I guess ours. To my knowledge, he went to work every day that he needed to, and as a partner in his retail wine and liquor business, he seemed to perform well. He was a warm, kindly man who, in retrospect, I could see was moody and self-doubting, although he was also handsome, charming, and creative. As the youngest of four, I felt that he was especially patient and attentive to me. I loved our excursions to the Lower East Side, where he had grown up, and trips to the Cloisters, Statue of Liberty, and Empire State Building to name a few. My friends, who also grew up in New York, rarely went sightseeing with their parents. With two friends of his, he founded a progressive Hebrew day school, because of his dissatisfaction with my public school experience and the available after-school Jewish religious educational opportunities. This was a major achievement in his life and one from which I benefitted. I attended the Akiba Hebrew Academy in the Bronx for several years until he had a disagreement with some of the other board members and precipitously withdrew me from the school. The school lives on, in part, to this day, merged with two others in the New York City area.

Naively, I had little appreciation, during my first thirty years of life, for how much the loss of my parents affected me. I protected myself from fully knowing those feelings and my family undoubtedly colluded in that effort by the absence of conversation about the topic of loss and the presence of a number of loving surrogate parents. Except for my intermittent and seemingly mild anxiety symptoms, which were by no means incapacitating, I had gotten used to my history. I did not talk about those parts of the family lore to most people, because they were embarrassing to me and seemed gruesome. When I did reveal them, it was in a seemingly rehearsed monologue. I had even thought about doling it out slowly to Dr. Adler. Instead, I just blurted it all out as historical facts, without much affect. I told him that he was thinking, "I'm going to have this guy on the couch for the rest of my life."

"Maybe that's your wish," he countered, like a good psychoanalyst.

"*Maybe now we could begin the treatment*," I thought, paraphrasing Philip Roth's last words in *Portnoy's Complaint*.

———

Well, I was prepared for the long haul, and he was right that I relished the thought that I could be reparented by a steady Dr. Adler, if only I could stay with him long enough, maybe forever! That idea was comforting in the early days of my analytic work, and predictably became less appealing after a few years and my increasing psychological self-awareness.

As the analysis progressed, I became sensitive to the daily efforts made to be a good boy, to do the right thing, to ward off the sadness of losses, to be sensitive to a disapproving look or comment from a supervisor, a friend, or even a department store salesperson. I realized how much psychic energy it required to be vigilant to protect myself from feeling hurt, embarrassed, or abandoned. I empathized with others whom I could see were using similar devices. The repetitiveness of the themes that dominated my inner life – feelings of great and unresolved loss, fears that nothing was as it seemed, and thinking that the world was a most uncertain place – made it difficult to know who I really was, although I was fully able outwardly to convey assurance and ease. I began to be able to explain dreams, musings, and situations that provoked the old anxieties and feelings of sadness. Much can be analyzed, understood, and put in perspective, but Dr. Adler also taught me, and it struck me as new information at the time, that there are some losses, traumas, missed opportunities, experiences, and events that leave permanent scars whose original causes can only be mourned, and they must be mourned in order to deal with them fully. Those losses may never be retrieved nor their absence fully healed, no matter how hard we try or how much we cry. With some effort, sometimes monumental, we come to know and try to accept those scars and carry on despite them or maybe even become stronger because of them. We can "build" healthier and happier experiences and relationships on top of them. And it is expectable, I have since learned that at some points in life they may become reactivated and be extremely painful again, when some provocative events, feelings, or memories reoccur. But then, hopefully, we can recognize them for what they are and say, "there it is again," and get past it by understanding and truly knowing their sources.

These realizations were incredibly helpful to me for my own well-being and as I began to treat more patients and became a better observer and therapist, for the people I was seeing who were dealing with themes of loss. As an association to this theme, I remembered a depressed woman whom I saw in my clinic in the air force. She was the wife of a pilot who had been killed when his fighter plane crashed in a training mission, twenty years earlier. She described a history of incredibly bad luck related to loss, including the death of her father, in his thirties, when she was just six. He had unfortunately stopped to buy groceries while the store was being robbed. He attempted to talk with the thieves about letting the customers go and was shot at point-blank range. And then at eighteen, she was beside her fiancé and witnessed him step off the curb into the street and be hit by a large truck, dying instantly. She said with great sadness, "Now that I'm older and suffer the loss of dependable good health and other disabilities of aging, I realize that the scars of all those other losses were additive and the feelings of grief were recurrent. They inflicted terrible, terrible wounds, permanently robbing me of some of the joy of life, but I've gone on anyway and have had a surprisingly good life." I was impressed with her sad realism, resilience, and strength despite the most catastrophic set of traumas I had heard to that point. She had lost three significant men in her life in three catastrophic events.

With increasing security, I began to know, through the analytic process, what I had missed, to mourn again and again and to more accurately assess who I was. Dr. Adler never flinched. In his quiet, softball way, he could handle himself and me, and I was reassured that he could handle anything that I could throw at him. He had become a steady part of my emotional world.

In earlier years, he had been a clinical director at Chestnut Lodge, a historic psychiatric hospital in Rockville, Maryland, near Washington, DC, that was described in the book *I Never Promised You A Rose Garden*. He had worked with Frieda Fromm-Reichman, Otto Will, Harold Searles, and other psychoanalytic "giants" of the time and had treated some very disturbed people. This was brought home to me one day, toward the end of my work with Dr. Adler, when I arrived slightly earlier than usual for my appointment. His office door was ajar, and I could hear him uncharacteristically shouting into the phone, "You've been bothering me with that crap for twenty years, Tom. Stop trying to manipulate me."

Is that a way for a psychoanalyst to behave? I thought. Glad, but also surprised and embarrassed, to have witnessed him in an unguarded moment, I commented as I lay down on the couch that he seemed a bit out of control. "Are you okay for the session?" I asked, half-jabbing at him but also wanting to check on his condition, for my own sake. I wanted to be sure he was still the stable guy on whom I had come to rely. I knew that I had both idealized him and, also at times, tried to shock him off the pedestal I built. Still obviously annoyed at Tom, he told me later in the session, after I had associated to the intrusion on our usually idyllic relationship, that this was an old Chestnut Lodge patient who he had not seen in twenty years but who calls him once or twice a year, utters chains of obscenities and various demands, and then hangs up. I felt good that he could get so angry, tell me about it, seem to recover, and move on. It was a lesson for me. We continued with my work.

7.

MR. WEISS

had been seeing Fred Weiss, weekly, for about three months. He routinely came to the office fifteen or twenty minutes before his appointment so he could sit in the waiting room and read the magazines that were collected there. He frequently commented on one or two of them as he entered the session and was disappointed if I had not already seen a particular article that interested him. Because he always tried to engage an exiting patient in conversation, I thought that another motive for his early arrivals may have been his desire to socialize with whomever he might meet in the waiting room, coming out of my office or that of my officemate. I sometimes could hear him attempting to broach a subject for comment or discussion, beyond the more usual nod, "hello" or "good morning" of other patients. All he could get from Ms. Burns was a rather perfunctory, quiet "good morning." She was clearly preoccupied after her visits, as were most of my patients.

Mr. Weiss was a sixty-seven-year-old man who had presented with persistent and overwhelming sadness over the loss of his older sister who had died from a massive stroke approximately one year prior to our first visit. In fact, he was dealing with losses accumulated over forty or more years, none of which had he fully mourned. As he had talked, during the first three or four sessions, about each of the significant, now deceased, people in his life, it seemed as though the wounds he suffered were still very fresh, although his parents had died twenty-five and thirty years ago, and his brother seven years ago. With the description of each loss and the circumstances of death, he had cried, with tears streaming voluminously down his wide, wrinkled, ruddy face. Mr. Weiss was a large man, six feet, two inches tall, weighing about 275 pounds, and looking as though he was not in great physical shape. His most striking features were his large, often twinkling, Mediterranean blue eyes, his wide, somewhat sardonic, smile, and his prominent abdominal paunch. After many tears were shed in the initial sessions, Mr. Weiss, or "Freddie," as he was known to friends and family, revealed himself to be an intelligent, extremely well-read, and highly cultured person. He was an avid museum-goer and theater and concert patron. He read and conversed in three languages and had played the piano for many years. Since childhood, he had always seen himself as a failure, and he offered no justification for that feeling. Although he graduated from City College and had a master's degree in English, Mr. Weiss always felt that he had not been successful in the work world and, in fact, had retired as soon as he could, at the age of sixty-two, from a mid-level administrative position with the city government. He told me that he was never ambitious, even from childhood, and more interested in his avocations, as he grew up, than in plans for a career. He thought of himself as a black sheep in his family because he had not had a profession, like his CPA brother, nor had he any immediate family, like his sister, who had been married and raised three children.

He sauntered into the office for his twelfth session, sat down in the chair, and with great ease and familiarity, stretched his legs out onto the matching tan leather ottoman and took a deep breath of satisfaction. My father would have said, "*He looked like he owned the place,*" I thought. It was just one side of Mr. Weiss. Today he was smiling. He had just been given two free tickets to Carnegie Hall by a neighbor, and he was ecstatic that he would be able to see and hear Isaac Stern perform, "and can you imagine, for nothing!" At moments like this, he felt as though he either had won a grand prize or had put something over on someone, or even stolen something he did not really deserve. Mr. Weiss had a wide range of affects. One minute he could be morbidly sad and crying, and the next he could exclaim exuberantly with a big grin across his large, friendly face. Melancholy had been his predominant mood for many years, maybe for most of his life. He liked to say, with some irony, "I've been depressed at least since my Bar Mitzvah, maybe since birth."

As his smile faded, he announced, "For months, since I've been coming here, I've been wanting to tell you more about my being queer." In my first session with him, Mr. Weiss had revealed the fact that he was gay and watched my face intently, seeming to expect me to be shocked, and quickly added, "Although I am technically bisexual, by history, at least. You know that I was even married to a woman, for a time?" He wanted to be special in all kinds of ways and said to me at that time, with great bravado, "I bet I'm the oldest Jewish fag you've treated or maybe even known. Maybe even the only one!" Although he could be rather provocative in his grandiosity and quite pathetic in his obvious feelings of inadequacy, I found Mr. Weiss to be an extremely likeable person, with a charm I found endearing. I suppose that was one reason I had initially agreed, because of his financial status, to see him at a significantly reduced fee, accepting what his insurance would pay, plus ten dollars directly from him.

"What else do you want to tell me about your being old and gay?" I asked.

"It's hard; hah, rather, it's difficult. I really only have Harry and we've been doing it for thirty years on and off, mainly blow jobs, some mutual masturbation, no anal stuff. I am too old for that shit, and besides, he seems to have become more dependent on his wife, who is a real bitch. I have become a big fat slob and I don't feel very sexy these days. I cannot attract anyone else in this shape. I don't even get a big charge out of jerking off, which I did regularly until four or five years ago. My old passions have given way to attempts at mere survival. That is what happens to a lot of old fags. And being an intellectual only gets you so far in this queer world!"

"You again sound lonely and sad that your relationships are so limited; do you feel helpless to do anything about it?" I said.

"You again sound like such a goddamn shrink; I can smell it a mile away. But I guess that's what I'm paying you for, or someone is paying for it," he countered with a knowing smile. "I'm part of the goddamn welfare system."

"Actually, being gay isn't so bad in your sixties. I get invited to a lot of fancy parties by old gals who need an extra man at the dinner table. I can carry on about Shakespeare, Picasso, James Joyce, Jane Austen, Henry James, and even Klimt and get a good meal, while minimally entertaining the old biddies to my left and right, some of whom aren't quite sure where they are and what the date is anyway. I manage well, even though I can barely get the old pecker up. I just need a blue or gray suit, occasionally a tux, that is clean, pressed, and in decent shape and a nice pair of black shoes. At times I have even been tempted to try something with some of the younger women at these events, but basically, I like flirting better than I like action anyway. I do get lonely, horribly lonely, and wish I had more friends, but then I'd also have more obligations; who needs them?"

"You obviously enjoy being with other people and you are good at it, but your worries about rejection seem to interfere with your making more attempts to socialize," I remarked.

"I sometimes think that if I didn't have Winkle, I'd kill myself," he said mournfully and provocatively. Winkle was his aged beagle who could now barely climb the stairs between Freddie's living room and bedroom. "Winkle loves me without any qualifications; he needs me as much as I need him, but for how long?" he added as his eyes pooled with tears. "I hope he drops dead before I do. I cannot put him to sleep, and I am worried that someone will if I go first. I still love carrying him upstairs, watching him eat and drink, and I treasure our short walks in the park. We are both decrepit. I guess that Winkle is my closest relative. I never had kids, at least that I know of, and my nieces really don't give a damn; they have their own lives and they are in California. And you, I'm paying you to be nice to me. You know what that makes *you*! It has been great to come here once every week, anyway, and I do think you like me. Anyway, I like you *a lot*." He wanted to be sure that I understood his emphasis on the last two words.

Mr. Weiss had never told his orthodox Jewish father about his sexual orientation, adding that "because I wasn't particularly effeminate, he never caught on. I would have loved to be able to let him know what I was dealing with; it would have been so abhorrent to him. But even though he was a bastard to me, I could not be that cruel," he blurted out with more than a hint of anger. His father had constantly berated him for his shortcomings in the work world, his lack of ambition, and before that, for his dreaminess and inattention to detail, especially around the grocery store the family operated on the Lower East Side.

"*You'll amount to nothing, nothing at all with that attitude,*" he imitated his father yelling at him with a thick Yiddish accent. It was clear that Freddie's father could not appreciate the many talents that his son did have and focused mostly on whether he would be able to adequately support himself in the future. He said that he always hoped that his father could be "a more normal American father, whatever that is. I guess I mostly hoped he would treat me better, be more respectful to me for who I was, even though I wasn't the son he envisioned having, and, as I said, he didn't even know the half of it."

He teared up as he felt the distress of not having a father who admired him, maybe even liked him. His mother, described by Freddie as a pleasant, rotund woman with large breasts and a cheery disposition, had tried to stand between father and son to prevent the verbal violence which frequently erupted, but she was mostly ineffectual in her efforts. She was kind but dominated by her husband in all respects.

Mr. Weiss used the therapy sessions for catharsis for his lifelong pain and to "buy" an attachment to a caring, supportive person called a therapist, who could also occasionally be an adept sparring partner, with no repercussions. He said that, periodically, he had "entered the mental health system to buy friends." Although he was often critical of me and disdainful of my lack of culture and experience in life, compared to his, he thought I would turn out to be the best psychiatrist he had seen, "maybe even better than Jacobs," the famous analyst and professor he had seen in Brooklyn twenty years earlier. I imagined that Mr. Weiss treated us all to similar critiques and compliments, and I did not let myself feel the full effect of either his praise or his condemnation.

Through various means, he tried to learn details of my private life and carefully watched my mannerisms, behavior, and reactions, particularly my reactions to his extremes of affect or outrageous exclamations. He wanted to gauge my tolerance, and indeed, my love, for him. He was confident that he knew many of my likes and dislikes and would frequently suggest books and movies that I "really must" read or see, expressing surprise that I had not already done so. He looked to me for approval and mostly tried to be a "good boy" to my role as attentive, nonjudgmental, supportive father, even though I was more than thirty years his junior. I tried to be steady and understanding. He was a man of enormous intellect, unfulfilled dreams, and great self-doubt, and he wanted continuous reassurance from someone that he was OK.

Today he also talked about several unsuccessful attempts to find part-time work. He had patrician tastes but barely supported himself on a modest pension and the interest and dividends from a small "nest egg." He was beginning to feel some financial strains, especially after the recent purchase of a new piano and a new air conditioner for his house and thought that "a part-time job would not terribly interfere" with his retirement.

"What do you think about my going back to work for the City?" he asked. "I've always wanted to be a librarian, to live and work with books. There are some jobs as library assistants advertised – essentially to organize and shelve books and that sort of shit. I am sure I could do it with my eyes closed. I could also hide out a little in the stacks, and maybe occasionally, even cop a feel off of some well-hung guy," he added provocatively. His face smiled with mischievous satisfaction and he looked to me for validation.

He tried so hard to be naughty, even perverse, but mostly succeeded at those times in showing me the little boy that Freddie was, even at age sixty-seven. He also hoped that being straight and relatively young, I might show some signs of embarrassment, and I am sure that I did, at times. That was one way he struggled with his competitive feelings toward me and other men. I suggested that he might like working in the library because of his love of literature and because he was basically a gregarious fellow. In that setting, he would encounter all sorts of people, and he could do one of the things he loved most – be an unabashed expert about books and literary history.

He welcomed my concrete support for his various endeavors, feeling quite insecure about making any decisions at this point in his life, maybe ever. I asked what he thought might be a possible downside to the library opportunity. He became anxious and admitted that maybe he would have a problem with the physical stamina required to be on his feet all day. He was sad that he was so out of shape at age sixty-seven. He had had a recent physical exam and his doctor told him to lose at least thirty pounds and to begin exercising daily. "I haven't gotten started on that program yet; maybe I want an excuse to fail at another thing in my life – even being a goddamn bookshelver."

I observed that he was fearful of new ventures, even ones such as this, which he obviously could handle and possibly really enjoy. Throughout his adult years, he had increasingly attempted to minimize demands put on him by others and, with few exceptions, had engaged in solitary activities. I thought that Mr. Weiss had been more depressed in the last month, with more reports of crying, less energy, more insomnia, and feelings of helplessness and hopelessness, which he attempted to partially hide with sarcastic and self-deprecating humor. He could not identify any reason for the increased sadness, except, "It's a real pain to be old."

I pointed out that sixty-seven was not really old and maybe there was another explanation for his recent "pain."

"That's easy for you to say; you're barely out of diapers," he countered, smiling and shaking his head adoringly at what he called my *baby face*. "I bet your old aunts loved to squeeze your *punim* ('face,' in Yiddish)," leaning closer to me, I thought, to gratify *his* wish to touch or even squeeze my cheeks. (How right he was about my old aunts!) Even in the short time I had seen him, he demonstrated his conflicted feelings about how familiar he could be with me.

He had been reluctant to take antidepressant medications in the past and had, in fact, discontinued the use of one he had been given by his general practitioner just before seeing me for the first time, because he thought it dried him out and made him constipated. I suggested that he might feel better taking some medication, and we might be able to titrate it a bit better to minimize negative side effects. His answer was, "Thanks for thinking of it; let's consider it next time." That was his stock answer for things he did not want to confront, and there were many.

I noted, to myself, from the early meetings with him, that Mr. Weiss always had trouble leaving the office. He would stand up when I said the session was over but continue to talk, shift from one foot to the other near my desk, ask a question, muse about the timing of the next session, or remind me about a play or movie to see or book to read that he had forgotten to mention during the session. He wanted to stretch out the time with me, and I felt that, at least in the early sessions, he would take a sharp limit as a rebuke. After a few weeks, I decided therefore to give him notice, about five minutes before the end of the session, so he could wind down. This served as a sometimes effective and relatively supportive device to set limits on his display of enormous needs.

It was apparent to me from the initial evaluation with him that Mr. Weiss did not want and would not benefit from analytically oriented work but that supportive psychotherapy and antidepressant medications could be useful to him. He had seen many psychiatrists since his early twenties, when he had been discharged from the army, after a year, with a psychiatric disability for an anxiety disorder. His pattern was to stay with them if they continued to be supportive and nurturing. He gave some evidence that, with each therapy experience, he attempted to mourn the loss of his hoped-for relationship with his father and the low self-esteem he felt from his earliest years. Whenever his therapists attempted to challenge him in some ways or analyze at a deeper level than he could tolerate, it sounded as if he left them.

He was a man with many personal and intellectual strengths, which could sometimes obscure his exceedingly fragile core and wounded self. The latter deficits had to be considered in every therapeutic intervention with him. While all the roots of his profound difficulties were still not entirely clear, his hunger for nurturing was evident, not only in his early and more recent life stories but also obvious in his relatively new relationship with me, in the treatment setting. Mr. Weiss's fragility was compounded by the fact that, except for one significant lover, a few inconstant friends, many acquaintances, and a string of psychiatrists to whom he sequentially attached, he had not successfully developed either intimate or supportive relationships, in which to celebrate successes and help cope with difficult life circumstances. He minimized Harry's value as a lover, and although he had mentioned having been briefly married to a woman, he avoided talking about his former wife or their relationship.

I was prepared to be a supportive figure in Mr. Weiss's life for the long haul. I was familiar with all his New York Jewish references to places and customs, his Yiddish phrases, and his exterior "wise guy" presentation. He was bright and charming but also needy. We could banter, a way of relating he enjoyed most. With some help, I thought he could do better in the last decades of his life, and I had looked forward to treating him.

———

Fred Weiss seemed somber and looked tired as he started what would turn out to be his last visit to my office. Pensively he said, "I had a dream last night that I was dying of some rare disease. The doctors had declared me terminal. Only Harry and you came to see me on my deathbed. I told you that I wanted to be cremated and my ashes spread somewhere, but I could not come up with a good place. I said that I would think of a place and hopefully let you know before I died. That sounds like me, doesn't it? I was philosophical about it, considering all the things I have told you about really having no one who cares whether I am alive or dead. Then, in the dream, I died and only two other people showed up for the funeral. I'm not sure who they were, but they certainly weren't the mayor and his wife."

"What do you think about the dream?" I asked.

"I think that I'm pretty damn depressed and lonely, and I don't give a fuck whether I live or die, and not many other people, maybe two, do either," he responded rather forcefully. "But do not worry, I'm not going to kill myself. Why now, you are going to ask me next? I am not sure, except that I realized that I'm spending money faster than I'm bringing it in. What if I outlive my money? I'm enjoying what I buy and I'm not really extravagant. Although, if you are poor, like me, everything is an extravagance. Yesterday I bought twenty-four tulip bulbs and some new gardening tools for my tiny patch of dirt that I call my garden, behind my house. I have also had a lot of indigestion. The nightly sip of Dewar's doesn't even taste as good as usual. So, I'm also worried that something is really wrong with my gastro system."

"You have seemed more depressed in the last month or so," I noted. "Your money problems don't strike me as the only cause of your increased distress. Your spending habits don't sound that different from what you've described earlier in our work. Can you think of other issues which may be depressing you; is this near a significant anniversary date?"

"I can't think of anything. Maybe it's the anniversary of my losing my virginity, but I haven't really kept track of that one; it was so long ago," he said smiling and reverting to his frequent provocative sarcasm of which he was still more than capable.

"You do have the capacity to enjoy many aspects of your life, including bantering with your psychiatrist, but when something saddens you, you fall quickly and feel as though there's little to live for," I countered. "You have so little reserve for the bad days."

"So, you think it would be a good idea for me to take some medicine to prevent me from jumping out of my second story window onto the grass below, when I quickly become despondent?" he offered, sarcastically again.

"I think that might be a good idea, not only for the particularly difficult times but also to improve the general quality of your life, about which you regularly complain," I continued. "It's not a panacea, but it might make living your life easier, maybe even enjoyable."

"The trouble with those medicines is they all dry you up like a prune. I don't need that now, especially with this queasiness I've been having."

"There are some that have fewer side effects, but you have mentioned your increased gastrointestinal upset several times recently. Since it is a good idea to have an EKG and some blood tests before starting on any of the antidepressants, you should see your internist for those and to check on those symptoms too."

"That's a very good idea," he exclaimed, pronouncing each word slowly and carefully, seemingly pleased that I was so concerned about his well-being. "I'll do that. It is good that I have a team of experts in my corner, and you're the leader; you're my rabbi."

Mr. Weiss went on to talk about his week at the library, noting his contacts with the "pieces of ass" with their "tight jeans and their spoiled precocious little kids," who frequented the children's section, and the group of old men with scuffed shoes and falling-down, mismatched socks, who spent every morning poring over the free *New York Times* or *Wall Street Journal* available in the reading room. "Those old guys will later be discovered to have stashes of dough under the mattresses," he said with some resentment. Once during each shift or so, someone asked him a question which challenged his intellectual prowess. He savored those interactions with a smart high school or college student or even a "Park Avenue dame" about whom he would again reveal his long-held prejudicial envy, "It's amazing how smart some of them can be, with their millions of dollars, and nothing to do all day." He teased the female librarians in his own outrageous ways until they blushed and/or hissed, with some budding affection, "Stop it, Freddie. It's enough already." In just a few months, he clearly had created a new family in his life, although he was quick to note that despite their library master's degrees, he knew more about literature, history, and just about everything else in the library than they ever would. But, he said, "They're good kids; we have a great time." With misplaced praise for me, he commented, "It was wise of you to push me into this library work," and I reminded him that it was *his* idea, which I supported. Although it now filled three or four pleasurable hours each day, when the library assistant time was over, he reverted to his chronically lonely, dejected persona, which seemed even more pervasively sad of late. He seemed less able to rise to an occasion that in the past would have briefly excited or rejuvenated him, even temporarily. I was concerned, although he had gone through periods like this in the past. I could not identify any new factors which might be responsible for his more profound despair. Despite having few supports, I did not think that he was a significant suicidal risk. Buying and planning to plant tulip bulbs which would bloom next spring was a hopeful sign. Our working alliance was strong, and I was confident that he would let me know if he became desperate. I verified that with him. Toward the end of the session, he spoke about an upcoming family gathering to which he was invited. He was ambivalent about going to "the affair" because among his cousins, he was regarded as somewhere between a "lovable eccentric" and a "black sheep." If he could be certain that he would feel comfortable, he would have relished the opportunity to socialize "with his people" and renew relationships with some distant relatives whom he rarely saw. But he had had enough of feeling like the poor soul for whom everyone felt pity, "especially me, I guess," he noted mournfully. "On the other hand, I should go to it. I have some good memories of some of these folks and you never know when one of them is going to drop dead, and then I'd really feel bad not to have seen them," he said with teary eyes. "I don't think that any of them are going to leave me a million bucks."

The session ended. After he left the office, I thought about Mr. Weiss's preoccupation with death, his dream, and his sense of impending doom. He always had this as background noise, but in this session, and in at least the preceding week, it had risen to greater prominence. I did not know what had recently changed to cause this; maybe this was just the ebb and flow of his chronic mood disorder.

He called to cancel the next session, saying it conflicted with his appointment with his internist whom he now felt increased urgency to see because he "really wanted to start on an antidepressant medication," and his abdominal pain had worsened. He said that he would call back to reschedule his appointment with me. It was unusual for him not to immediately ask me for alternative dates and times. I waited a day and then called him. He was not at home, and I left a message on his answering machine with some options for appointment times. He failed to return my call in the next three days, also uncharacteristic of him. I became more concerned. I did not know the last names of his nieces nor any of his friends.

After five days, he left a message saying that he was in New York Hospital for some tests and he would call back to reschedule his appointment as soon as he knew when he was getting out, maybe in a day or two. He called on the second day, at a time when I had ten minutes between patients, and I could answer the phone. With a tired voice he said, again pronouncing each word slowly and with emphasis, "Am I glad to have reached you. I am very sick. I have cancer of the pancreas and I'll be dead in six weeks."

For a moment I thought, *there's Freddie doing it to me again*, but then I realized that this was no banter, no provocative joke. I felt sad, almost tearful myself, and without thinking said, "That's bad news. I am very sorry to hear that news. Are you still in the hospital? May I come to see you?"

"I'd like that, but you'd better hurry. That last dream may come true quickly. Seriously, I very much want you to visit me. When can you come?"

"I'll be there later this afternoon, between four and five."

I thought about Mr. Weiss seeming to have been increasingly depressed in the last month or so. Was that the effect of the growing pancreatic cancer? The association between depression and certain cancers was known, but I had only seen it this dramatically once, and in that case, there were coincident psychotic symptoms and pancreatic cancer. The acute psychosis had, in that patient, preceded the diagnosis of the cancer by about a month. In Freddie's case, it was difficult to discern any association because his prevailing mood was chronically depressed.

Lying in bed in a semi-private room in a part of the hospital that could have been fifty years old or more, Freddie Weiss looked considerably older, weaker, and sadder than when I had seen him in my office less than two weeks earlier. He greeted me with, "Isn't the unconscious something? Here I had this dream about dying a week or two ago and now I am doing it. It's amazing." (Heavy emphasis on the second syllable.)

Initially, I was speechless and then managed, "I'm very sorry. I hope that I can help you through these next months."

"We've had a good run, you and me – short but sweet. You have made this last year or so easier than I thought life could be, especially at this age and with this unsexy body. This is a hell of a way for me to terminate treatment with you, but at least you will remember this one. Maybe you'll write an article, a book, or something about it someday?"

I was impressed by the consistency of his banter, and I did think that maybe I had made some very short-term difference in his life, although I knew that dying people were prone to hyperbole, and Mr. Weiss was particularly susceptible to that.

"I certainly will remember you, but you are not dead yet so we should not bury you. There are undoubtedly still things for us to talk about. Do you want to tell me what's happened since I last saw you?"

He began to describe the last ten days in meticulous detail, being notably laudatory about the internist and surgeon he had seen and their care and consideration in making the diagnosis and fully informing him of its implications. "The bottom line is that I will be dead in six weeks and somehow I think that they'll be right. They seemed to know their stuff." ("Knowing their stuff" was one of the supreme compliments that Freddie could bestow on someone.)

"How do I feel, you were next going to ask? I am OK. I have had a strange but full life, and realistically, I do not have much that keeps me looking forward. In a way, it is a relief. I could have had a happier time, but who said life was guaranteed to be happy? It is a struggle for many people, maybe for most who are honest enough to admit it. With a lot of help, I have mostly stayed in there fighting. You know the name Erik Erikson, don't you? And about his stages of development?"

Freddie was teaching or testing me again, even at this desperate moment in his life, I thought. "Yes."

"Well, I've won the struggle at most of those eight stages, and even the last one, *integrity versus despair*, I think I have mastered it without too much despair. Occasionally, I have drifted back to an earlier level, but the beauty of Erikson is that he allowed for that," Freddie said, teaching me about one of my psychoanalytic heroes.

"I think that you have done pretty well and even enjoyed yourself, in spite of many obstacles."

"Obstacles is a nice way of saying a pretty fucked up life, although there have been many people and experiences that I have been able to enjoy. I never really described to you how much I used to enjoy sex. I loved it, with men and with women. You may not think of me as a sexy guy, but I would not mind if that was on my tombstone – "Freddie Weiss, A Sexy Guy." But it has been years, and there are other things that could be on my tombstone. How about, 'He loved James Joyce?'"

"You have many attributes and loves to put on the list. They are some of the reasons you loved life. I'll leave now; you look tired, and I must go back to the office. I'll come back in a day or two."

"Please do. Time is short."

I left the hospital naively bewildered at, and rather in awe of, the cycle of life and death. I thought about the dozen or so babies I had delivered in medical school. I remember thinking then that each new birth was a fantastic miracle, all their parts usually working in harmony and opening the possibilities of a lifetime ahead. And, on the other end of the spectrum, there is the finality of death. An inexorable course was now set for Mr. Weiss. It was a powerful force of nature – "Who shall live and who shall die." The liturgy with which both Freddie and I were familiar rang in my ears. Although I had witnessed a considerable number of deaths, both personally and professionally, it had been years. I had not lost a patient since I was in the air force and, if it is possible, I had then become somewhat inured to the notion that a significant percentage of severely injured and maimed war casualties sent back from Vietnam would die. I felt more tender these days, probably because of deaths close to me in the family, and the notion of Fred Weiss dying, and dying quickly, was very upsetting to me. He had had little support at any time in his life, and in the next weeks or months, there was no reason to think that much more would be mobilized. That would be difficult for him, and possibly for me.

I returned to the hospital two days later and then again, a week after that. Mr. Weiss appeared weaker each time but was pain-free thanks to the considerate administration of analgesics by his physicians. His was a vicious cancer, wasting him before our eyes. At about three weeks, he wanted to go home, to die. He had to "settle his affairs" and he "wanted to die in his own bed, surrounded by the few people who mattered." He wanted me to see him in his home, a duplex he owned on the edge of Hell's Kitchen, on the West Side. He said somewhat devilishly, "Under ordinary circumstances, you couldn't be seduced into a patient's apartment, but I found this ingenious way of getting you there. Sorry I can't make you a gourmet meal. I would have *really loved* to do that."

The next day, I walked up the stairs of the run-down four-floor building that had been oddly divided into duplex apartments but retained the decrepit ambiance of decades in a gang-torn section of the city. Someday, I thought, this area would be developed into fancy condos and cute restaurants and bars. I knocked on the door and a woman whom I estimated to be in her mid-sixties responded. She introduced herself as Annette, a neighbor in the building. I was ushered up to Freddie's bedroom, where he lay in maroon silk pajamas, propped on three or four pillows, with a white sheet pulled to his chest. He smiled faintly and limply put out his right hand. I barely touched it, when it faded from my loose grip, fatigued with illness.

"The move from the hospital has worn him out," Annette offered. "The picture on the wall behind you is for you to have, Doc," he whispered, "Hang it in your house or in the office. It's a photo I took of the Statue of Liberty on a foggy day. That is where I want my ashes scattered, between Ellis Island and the Statue, where my parents, and I'd guess yours, came from Europe to the Lower East Side."

I thought that, if nothing else, Freddie had built a positive relationship with me, and maybe he had gained something from that. In a strange way, so had I. That is so much of what psychotherapy is about for many, maybe most, patients. He was exhausted by these few sentences and closed his eyes. His chest heaved slowly and rhythmically. I looked around the room, which was decorated with antique furniture, piles of books, and several paintings and framed photographs, with the signature "FW" in the corner of each. He had not told me much about his interest in photography.

Another woman, Florence, probably in her late fifties, approached me from the living room and quietly said that she worked with Freddie in the library. She had come to love his sense of humor, "the twinkle in his beautiful blue eyes, and his boyish manner." She had come over to help him on her day off. She said, "It's hard to believe that he's talking about his ashes and we are not protesting."

I nodded in agreement, but I knew the devastating course of Freddie's illness. This was indeed a strange but remarkable way to be able to terminate a therapeutic relationship, I thought. I wanted to roll up my sleeves and help the women in some concrete way, but I felt awkward, so I moved back to the side of the bed and held Freddie's hand for a minute, while he dozed. As I let it go, he opened his eyes and offered weakly, "See you around, Doc."

I thought he would die in the next few days, and I wanted to come back there before that happened. In a mystical way this seemed like a holy place, not Jewish holy, just holy. Maybe that is what death is up close – strange, mystical, and holy? I returned in two days and Freddie was in a coma but breathing on his own. I wanted to have one more exchange with him, but that part of him was gone. I stared at him as he lay in bed with what I thought was a slight sardonic smile on his face. I left after some conversation with Annette, the neighbor. I told her how important I thought her care of Freddie had been during these last days. With tears streaming down her face, she said, "I loved him like the big brother I lost to the Nazis." Sobbing, she lunged at me and threw her large arms around my neck in a firm hug. I patted her on the back and feeling more like Freddie's rabbi than therapist at that moment, I said, "I'm sure he understood your feelings for him." I was surprised that he had never mentioned her to me. She obviously had become a good friend to him.

Annette called me the next morning and told me that Freddie had died during the night, peacefully, in his sleep. I thanked her for her caring.

Annette called a week later to tell me that they were scheduling a "ceremony" to spread Freddie's ashes near the Statue of Liberty in the next several days. Some others from the library, his friend Harry, and a few of his neighbors would be there. They were planning to go out on one of the public boats to Liberty Island, bringing lunch from a local deli that Freddie frequented, and with little ceremony and no speeches, spread the ashes. He had not ever mentioned most of the people who would attend, except Harry, in our sessions. I was already quite affected by his death, more drained than I would have anticipated, and chose to mourn privately, and I did. I felt sad that Freddie had to conceal so much of his life from the people closest to him, particularly his shame within his family, his fear of not being accepted. I was glad that there would be more than two people at his memorial event, although Freddie obviously would not know that. (As was typical of him, he had underestimated his impact on the people around him.) I thanked Annette for her consideration in calling, and again, for her extraordinary attentiveness to Freddie in his last days. I hung Freddie's Statue of Liberty picture in my office.

8.

MR. KENT

Charles Kent was a fifty-two-year-old married man whom I had been seeing for three months, initially at the insistence of his wife. She had "had it with him because of his increasingly erratic behavior."

Over the year prior to his first visit to my office, she noticed his becoming increasingly irritable at home, with mood swings that varied from his being rather exuberant in expressing his ideas, often in what seemed to her to be an inappropriately loud voice and with dramatic gesticulations, to being unusually somber, even tearful, about things that didn't seem to warrant so much affect. His mood swings each lasted somewhere between four and six weeks, sometimes less, according to his wife, who had insisted on accompanying him to his first visit with me. She reported that he frequently was late coming home from the office, and more than occasionally had alcohol on his breath. Although he had apparently been able to carry out his responsibilities at work, she thought, there were times, possibly once or twice per month, when he just could not get out of bed in the morning because he was so depressed. He would call his secretary to say he was taking the morning off or he would make up an excuse about some meeting he had in New Jersey. Noting that the changes in her husband were growing in intensity over the year prior to his initial visit with me, his wife had been increasingly concerned that "something was really wrong with him." She feared that he would jeopardize his career in the public relations/development firm, of which he was a partner and where he was both highly regarded and rather successful, earning $200,000 or more per year over the past five years, as a fundraising specialist. She also felt that their marital relationship had deteriorated, and she was now "walking on eggshells" lest she upset him and cause him to be more irritable. Their sex life had diminished significantly because he was either "too tired and didn't feel like it" or he was agitated and would stay up far later than the time she would go to bed. She wondered whether he was depressed, whether he had become a substance abuser, whether he was having an affair, or possibly he was just dissatisfied with some part of his life, maybe their marriage, and was unable to express whatever it was. He had never been one to readily express feelings. Although she confessed to being psychologically naive, she knew that something had drastically changed and visiting a psychiatrist seemed like a good place to start. She had called her husband's internist a few weeks before she had gotten her husband to call me, but the internist passed off Mr. Kent's moods as "something men can go through in midlife." That did not seem right to her.

While generally seen as a clever, often witty fellow at work and in social situations, Mr. K. told me that he "held his emotional cards close" and used his personality as a "buffer to the world." His father and grandfather had been that way and he guessed he "had inherited the gene for that." He had added that the one emotion his father expressed freely was anger. Reluctantly, he had admitted, after his wife had retreated to the waiting room in the first session, that he noted the changes his wife described, but he thought that she exaggerated them. He would not have sought treatment, at least not when she urged him to do so. While he initially attempted to "hold his cards close" with me too, using a glib, off-putting approach, after several sessions he talked more openly about several difficult issues. He acknowledged that he had a "fascination, indeed an obsession, with women, particularly young, beautiful, and slightly gritty ones with shapely bodies." At least once per week, he would arrange a visit from a "call girl" to his office or to a local hotel room. Since his wife was used to his being late, because he often entertained clients for dinner, he frequently arranged these "visits" to occur in the early evening. The women were usually young, attractive people who sometimes said they were working their way through college or professional school. Because of his regular use of a particular escort agency, he often requested and got to know two or three women quite well and felt that he had developed significant relationships with them. He had the fantasy that one or two even loved him. Nonetheless, he never objected to giving them the two or more hundred dollars that it cost him for a few hours of their company, and they never refused the extra tip he would give them when he felt ebullient and generous. He acknowledged that each woman had an obviously tough or "gritty" side to her and that they would not otherwise be doing this kind of evening work.

When he was feeling well, and especially when he was euphoric, he engaged in passionate sex, having intercourse with the call girls, he said, at least several times in each encounter. He boasted about his stamina. On other occasions, particularly when he was depressed, he would just want to lie next to the woman and have her gently stroke him, while having "light conversation." He felt soothed and was convinced that they really cared about him. He felt guilty about his activity with the prostitutes but rationalized that it was separate from his relationship with his wife, which he regarded as "stable, if not passionate." His sex life with his wife was "OK. You know how it is after twenty years," he offered in the spirit of male camaraderie with me. A recent event had slightly alarmed him, but he maintained that even after it occurred, he did not think anything was "really wrong" with him. He had gone to an upscale Third Avenue bar and restaurant with some of "the girls" from the office to celebrate his secretary's birthday. "After several drinks and possibly a few hits of marijuana," he climbed up on the bar, began dancing, and then unbuttoned and dropped his pants to "moon" the assembled crowd. He described the episode as a "fun, impulsive thing." Fortunately, a partner of his happened to be having dinner in the adjoining restaurant section, hearing the commotion and laughter that ensued, rescued him from the bar, helped him zip up his pants, and had him taken home by one of his associates. On his return home, with some assistance from his co-worker, he told his wife that he just had too much to drink but left out the "gory" details. The next day he had a bad hangover and was mortified at having to face "the girls" on his arrival in the office. He wondered if his father had done things like that, because now that he thought about it, his father was "a fairly erratic fellow." Frank Kent had been a marine officer who worked his way up to colonel during World War II and was known to be a tough-talking, rough-around-the-edges kind of guy. After retirement from the marines, he worked as a car salesman in several dealerships, with a good deal of financial success. He regularly berated his wife and children and "took the belt to all of us."

Mr. Kent winced at his memories of being chased out the backdoor by his six-foot, five inch, overweight, enraged, out-of-control father. "It was like a train with a head of steam rolling through, and you just had to get out of his path as fast as you could." He was never quite sure what got his father so angry, but he knew to flee from the environment. "When the storm hit," Charlie would jump on his bicycle and disappear for hours, returning to familiar paths in the various parks in his neighborhood and others nearby in the North Bronx, allowing him the comfort of solitary reverie he could achieve in no other way. Invariably he would return home to find it a quieter place, with his father gone or passed out from fatigue or booze. His mother was a substantial person, a now-retired and respected Latin and French teacher at a Bronx high school, and although she could maintain discipline in her classes, her husband's propensity for violence scared her and frequently sent her seeking refuge behind a locked door in another part of their house. Charlie was not sure what happened to his younger sisters in these episodes of terror. "It was each person for himself." It was obvious that they were all scarred by their early experiences. One sister became a corporate executive but was disabled with ulcerative colitis which forced her to have most of her colon removed and to live with a colostomy, from age thirty-five. The other suffered with a severe anxiety disorder with phobias, obsessive/compulsive symptoms, and panic attacks, none of which responded to treatment very well. She had become a virtual recluse.

Charles Kent was a likeable, bright, rather charismatic but clearly self-doubting man who had done well in his work and family life until recently. He had attended Stuyvesant High School and then excelled academically and socially at Brown. He had intellectual interests, having majored in philosophy, and was gregarious and charming. A family friend had helped him derail his plans to go to graduate school and instead steered him toward becoming a development specialist, raising money for large nonprofit organizations and universities. Everyone who knew him said he was "a born salesman"; he seemed always to be "on." It was difficult now for his associates to see him as having been a potential philosopher or professor. Through the veneer he had cultivated, I saw both his charm and his vulnerability and felt him trying to fend me off, something he apparently did, emotionally, with most people. He tried to present himself as a "good ole boy," with a persistent public smile, hearty, firm handshake, and a pat on your back. Because of his recent erratic behavior, I wondered whether he would stay around long enough for an assessment and the beginning of any treatment

I had initially decided to meet with him weekly and see where we would go in an extended evaluation, trying to understand his early life history, the effects of a violent father, and a mother who "meant well" but was largely ineffectual within the family setting, because she too was a victim of her abusive husband. It was not clear who, if any, were the important people in his emotional life from his early days to the present, but he obviously had many strengths garnered from somewhere. And then there was the question of his biological predisposition to what sounded like a cyclical mood disorder. There was no evidence of his ever having a significant manic episode nor apparently had his father, but it was clear that both definitely had mood swings, and possibly worse. They were both vulnerable to excesses and irritability which could be called hypomanic, and both drank large amounts of alcohol, possibly to "treat" their unstable moods.

I reviewed the medication possibilities in my mind and did not feel that tranquilizers, antipsychotics, or antidepressants were indicated immediately and initially doubted that they would now be helpful to him. Lithium carbonate had become a popular treatment, as a mood stabilizer, for pro-phylaxis and treatment of manic-depressive disorder in the four or five years before I first saw him. Some of my colleagues were already using lithium for these kinds of milder mood swings or cyclothymic states and reported significant stabilization of patients' behaviors, but that wasn't an indication that was yet generally accepted. Things would change dramatically in this area of psychopharmacology of mood swings over the next ten years, with the advent of new antidepressants, improved antipsychotic medications, and new mood stabilizers that had their origins as anticonvulsants. Mr. Kent had made it clear from the outset of my work with him that he did not want to have his "brain all screwed up with medication." This was not an uncommon view among patients I had seen with cyclical mood swings, although the irony of their substantial self-medication with alcohol was striking, and their brains were frequently already "screwed up" as a result of that "home remedy."

I wondered what, if any, transference feelings would emerge. Sometimes when a patient is cautious divulging the content of feelings and thoughts, the relationship that evolves in the treatment room is a useful vehicle for both therapist and patient to understand what is not otherwise being dis-closed. Although I was twenty years his junior, I thought it was likely that he would relate to me as an authority figure and feel the punitive as well as wished-for supportive aspects of a parental relationship. I wondered about possibly seeing him more regularly with his wife, both to get a more hon-est and complete view of his range of behaviors and moods and to break through some of the denial he had about the signs and symptoms he was demonstrating outside of my office.

We met together for several months, and gradually more emotionally laden material came out. He specifically requested that I not talk to his wife after the initial visit nor have her join us in any future sessions. Mr. Kent had increasing difficulty containing his hypomanic behavior and the early work in psychotherapy seemed to have little effect on his symptoms. On at least one occasion, he said he did not feel like sitting in the chair during our

session. He just wanted to walk around the room so he "could think better."
He was agitated. Over time I saw that his disorder was obviously cyclical
and regular in its pattern. He had depressive periods alternating with hypomanic episodes every four to six weeks, almost exactly, with essentially no
level period between the highs and lows. The depressive episodes were of
significant intensity but never psychotic in nature. He would be sad, enjoy
nothing, have decreased energy, insomnia, and decreased appetite, but he was
never suicidal and was able to function, although at times quite marginally.
In my office, he talked more slowly and had a paucity of ideas, with many
silences. During the hypomanic weeks, he was energized, variably euphoric,
highly productive, even if occasionally scattered and irritable, needing only
three or four hours of sleep per night. He was witty and fast-talking in our
sessions. He showed no evidence of delusions, hallucinations, paranoid
thoughts, or other psychotic symptoms. He had come to realize that he
should schedule important client meetings during the energized "up" weeks
rather than during the dreary "down" times, when he had diminished focus
and was able to get little accomplished. His sexual appetites and behaviors
were exaggerated during the hypomanic phases and substantially diminished
when he was depressed. In both phases, in addition to the evening call girl
visits, he frequented strip joints in the seamy parts of town at lunchtime
and occasionally between appointments. His judgment about possibly being
seen by clients or colleagues was clouded. During one session, in which he
appeared to be moderately depressed, he started with a description of some
sad memories about feeling "on his own" during his childhood years. For
the first time since I had been seeing him, he expressed his connection to
me. With some tearfulness, he said, "I'm grateful to have someone who is
so attentive and interested in me. I have never had anyone like that in my
life. I've had no friends or family members who really knew me." He also
admitted that at times during the last hypomanic episode he felt "on the edge"
more than he ever had, and he was worried that he might "flip out and go
crazy." He frightened himself a bit by expressing that, and he did not want
to explain further adding, on second thought, "I'm sure I can handle it."

Either his illness was advancing in severity or he was being more open about admitting to the symptoms that had been present for some time. Rather than pursue some of the sad material lurking just below the surface, I thought I should seize the moment and review the possibility of medication with him again. I tried to educate him more directly about the cyclical nature of his disorder and its potential to become a full-blown manic-depressive illness. He was strongly opposed to any psychotropic medications that might change the "up" periods, and he did not think the depressing weeks were so terrible.

"I know how to schedule myself. I don't want to be doped up with that crap," he emphasized again. When I referred to the potential usefulness of lithium, "That stuff is for nut cases," was his retort. My further attempts to talk with him about the reality of medication treatment were met with increasing opposition. The cyclical nature of his disorder had become obvious to me, and the hypomanic episodes seemed to be getting more florid and potentially dangerous. A trial of lithium was clearly indicated, I thought. At that point in my career, I had initiated medication treatment in only a few manic-depressive patients outside of a hospital setting. It was worth a try in view of his escalating symptoms.

Charles did not want to lose his "edge" as a salesman; he feared that his charm and his wit might be dulled. Like many manic or hypomanic people, he questioned why he should take a medication that would limit his energy, ebullience, and creativity. I was increasingly concerned that his swings, although reliably cyclical with essentially no truly level periods, were becoming more severe in amplitude, and with time, and no one could predict when, his hypomania could explode into a more out-of-control mania, and his depressions could become the devastating black moods that might immobilize him. They could, in fact, be lethal, although he denied that he had ever thought seriously about suicide.

I liked treating manic patients; they felt familiar to me. For the relatively short time that I had been in practice, I had had some good experiences with them and felt a personal dedication to their treatment. I knew that I had to be careful not to overread these situations because several members of my own family had mood disorders in an era when certain medications, such as lithium carbonate, were not yet available. As I thought about the few months I had been seeing Charles, I realized that we had spent a lot of time repetitively going over the same material, particularly concerning his symptoms and my thoughts about medication. It was a persistent, but cordial, tug of war that I did not want to lose, because I knew, firsthand, from patients and family, what the consequences of this illness could be.

I pointed out to him that lithium was different from other psychotropic medications. It was a salt, like sodium and potassium, and probably would not "dope him up" in the small doses I would prescribe. It would require periodic blood draws to check on drug levels in his system. A small number of patients reported adverse effects with the relatively low dosages and low blood levels with which we would start. While it was not a panacea, I thought it might help him feel less out of control and allow him to function more evenly and reliably, with less energy consumed in planning his life around his disorder and with possibly less risk of his disorder escalating to psychotic proportions.

"What are you going to do if I refuse the drug?" he challenged. "Will you forcibly hospitalize me or kick me out of treatment?" he persisted.

I responded that, for now, neither of those options seemed appropriate. I noted to myself that he had some concerns about jeopardizing our relationship, and he was also trying to assess how alarmed I was about his state.

I strongly urged him to try the medication for a month or two with the caveat that although the beneficial effects might not be completely apparent by then, he would have some indication of adverse effects if they were to occur. He reluctantly agreed to start on a small dose of lithium carbonate. He bargained for the lowest possible dose and I cautioned that we would likely increase it very slowly as we measured its effects and blood levels. Since he was quite strong-willed and controlling, in general and about the idea of medication, specifically, I took his capitulation to be some reluctant self-recognition of his increasing disability and its effect on his daily functioning. In addition, he possibly heard my continuing concern and frustration about optimally treating him, and he may have come to some grudging respect for that.

———

Charles had taken a minimal, and clearly a less than therapeutic, dose of lithium carbonate for about two weeks. He opened a session with, "I'm done with that stuff; I couldn't stand it. I stopped it yesterday. I felt as though my head was filled with cotton. I could not think straight and did not feel in control of myself. At that rate I would not be able to raise a dime for my clients," he protested, "and where will that get me, or you?"

It was difficult to get an exact accounting of the adverse effects of the lithium that he experienced, but I was convinced that I would have to be an exceptional salesman, or he would have to be significantly more disabled, if there was going to be a next time for taking one of those pills. Even though I was quite sure that he would benefit from a mood stabilizer, I did not want the issue of lithium to become a barrier in our relationship. Since there was little or no chance that I would get him to a therapeutic level of medication soon, I decided to temporize, observe him carefully, establish a firmer alliance, and watch for the possible escalation of symptoms, both depressive and manic, which, in view of his recent pattern, seemed inevitable. I thought it was important to have his wife more involved, but Mr. Kent reinforced his objection to being "baby-sat" in the therapy by her.

"How was your week, otherwise?" I asked, after his declaration to be medication-free.

"I'm OK and I'm not shitting you; you don't have to bring my wife in to verify everything," he said loudly and rather defensively, and with more disinhibition and defiance than I had heard in his speech until now. I thought that he increasingly sounded like some of his descriptions of his father.

I attempted to refocus our work, so that I would be surer that he would be honest with me and not think that I was interested only in having him "doped up."

"Even though I feel that you would, over time, do well with lithium, I don't want that to be a continuing struggle between us," I commented. "I hope that you'll be able to talk freely about your moods, thoughts, and feelings. If that is not possible, our work together will certainly lose considerable value. We can put the medication issue on hold for now."

"I'm OK with that, now that I set you straight on what I will and won't do," he said with a wry, but triumphant smile.

"I see that you feel much more comfortable when you are in control."

"You're right, and having bought into seeing a psychiatrist, I'm a little worried about becoming too dependent on you and, I guess, losing control."

"What does that mean?"

"I don't want to depend on anyone. I run my own life pretty well, although I am certainly a victim of my moods, to some extent. The 'ups' are fun, exciting, charged, and except for that time when I mooned the folks in the bar, I have never gone too close to the edge. The 'downs' are not fun, but I can tolerate them. Maybe you could give me some medication for *those* times?"

This was the first time that he had spontaneously mentioned the "ups and downs" and the first time he had made even a veiled request for medication. Maybe he was expressing some increased ambivalence about his treatment. I could not push drugs again with him, at least not right now. I took a realistic and educative approach to the subject.

"I can't give you antidepressants, just for occasional use, for a month or two at a time, because it usually takes that long for them to be effective. In addition, there is a chance that antidepressants, without coverage with a mood stabilizer, might make you quite manic and out of control. We shouldn't risk that." (There was already considerable clinical evidence showing, particularly in patients who were susceptible to manic symptoms, that a manic episode could be precipitated by taking antidepressants without the benefits of a mood stabilizer, such as lithium.)

"Well, I can muddle along for a while. I'm kind of used to it. By the way, I had a dream last night, for the first time since I've been seeing you. Do you discuss dreams?"

I was impressed by his naiveté or possibly pseudo-naiveté, which he had not evidenced in earlier sessions. His question had a childlike quality. I suspected that my backing off on the medication issue had made him feel slightly more trusting of me and, indeed, possibly more able to acknowledge his feelings of dependency, about which he was so fearful. I also wondered whether he was frightened that he had "won" the battle over medications and the thought that maybe I would be less interested in treating him, or even give up on him.

"We can talk about whatever you want. Dreams sometimes give us information about thoughts and feelings that we might not otherwise easily understand."

"In this dream I breathlessly run into the teeming emergency room of a hospital and lying on a gurney in one of the stalls was a large body, completely covered with a white sheet. My thought was that the man had just died and was about to be wheeled to the morgue, but because of the number of patients in the ER, no one had gotten around to doing it. I overheard someone, maybe an intern or resident, saying to a more senior doctor that they had tried to revive the guy, but it was hopeless; he never had a chance. That's all I remember of it, but I woke up with a start, sweating, scared, not sure whether it really happened or not. Maybe there was more to it that I don't remember."

"What are your thoughts about the part of the dream that you do remember?"

"The form under the sheet was about the size of my father, and when my father died, I did have to go to the morgue to identify his body. He had collapsed and died on Broadway, possibly of a heart attack, but he also had been drinking a lot and had a lot of alcohol in him. I am not sure why I would be dreaming about my father now; he's been dead for ten years. He didn't even get worked on much in the ER; he was pretty much dead on arrival. I'm also not sure why I was so scared with this dream."

"Sometimes dreams have several threads and multiple origins or meanings. Even though you initially thought the body was that of your father, it could also stand for somebody or something else."

"OK, I get it. I am just a little smaller than my father, so maybe it was me on that gurney. Maybe because of the wild side of me, I will end up dead in a hospital emergency room after doing something stupid, like mooning the crowd in the bar, or worse? But then who was that running into the ER?"

I was struck that for a college graduate in philosophy, Charles was again sounding quite concrete, maybe defending against possible meanings or symbols in the dream. I wondered whether this was a denial of what seemed to me to be rather apparent, or was it the product of his underlying disorder? Was he having some difficulty with his cognitive processes?

I asked if he had any associations to the other people in the dream. He could not think of any. I continued, "So you have a person, maybe your father, maybe you, lying dead on a gurney and two doctors discussing his (your) lack of responsiveness to the attempts to keep him (you) alive. It's a busy hospital ER and you rush in on this scene and, at least on awakening, feel very frightened."

"That's a reasonable summary. You know, I'm really not that good at this."

"You are a bright guy who reads people pretty well in your work. At Brown you took courses that involved a considerable amount of abstract thinking. So possibly your difficulty analyzing this dream is self-protective, maybe because the material is so uncomfortable to look at." I realized that I was feeling and sounding a bit testy with his inadequacy, possibly also annoyed and anxious that he was resistant to my efforts to properly treat him with medication.

"I also took a couple of psych courses way back then and used to love analyzing my dreams and those of my roommates and girlfriends. I was rather good at it then, but where did that get me?"

Because Charles was able to look at this dream only in the most obvious ways, I decided to continue to suggest some basic ideas that I thought were contained in the dream. I didn't want to lose what I considered important material and thought that I might also be able to assess his reaction to my interpretations of it. I also was aware that this was a rare opportunity for us to work together, when the sessions so far had not been particularly collaborative.

"It seems to me that the dream *is* about you, in both roles. One way to see it is as a review of what you went through with your father and your distress about his loss. Quite correctly you ask, 'Why now?' Maybe the 'now' has to do with your present state. Although you sometimes resist acknowledging it, like your father, you are feeling less stable than usual and dealing with the disability of a mood disorder. There is a risk that it could kill you too. The doctors, one or combination of which may be me, said that they couldn't help your father (you); he (you) didn't respond to their efforts. It was too late; he was essentially dead on arrival. I can see where that would be scary to you. I think the dream then is about a number of things – your identification with and feelings about your father, your own mood problems, and also about the treatment with me here, how adequate we are in the treatment process, and what will become of you."

"So you are trying to tell me that we are back to lithium again – my recognition of my need for treatment versus my fear of it?"

"Not only lithium but treatment in general and working on other issues in your past history and current life – all about what makes you the way you are."

"Can you help me out a bit more on this? I'm not sure I get it."

"The fragment you described has some elements beyond your concerns about your father. I am struck by a few things that we have not talked about much. You describe running in 'breathlessly,' which might be a metaphor for a manic, somewhat out of control, state. The doctors are busy, don't even have time to wheel the body to the morgue, which is rather extraordinary. Bodies are not usually left hanging around the ER on gurneys, except after a mass disaster. You might ask, 'Who will take care of me? On whom can I depend?' And then there is the whole issue of your getting treated properly and by whom? Is there hope for you? Do *you* have a chance? You are frightened by those questions."

"Wow, you certainly milked every word of that," he said with apparent amazement.

I did feel on my game. I noted to myself that Charles' bravado of the early sessions, and even early in this hour, was gone, or at least significantly diminished, and he related to me, especially in reference to the dream, much more as an early adolescent relating respectfully to a knowing and caring parent. I resisted commenting on his use of "milked," although the dependency issues in the dream and in the transference were becoming more apparent. After several months of supportive treatment, I was surprised that he revealed such a transparent dream, but he could not really work on it. Rather, he accepted my analysis of it, passively, without rejecting or even modifying the possible meanings I laid out.

At the end of the session, he seemed calmer than I had seen him before, and I had the feeling, for the first time, that maybe we were developing some working alliance. Maybe Charles had new respect for his own unconscious, and I had gotten some credit for being able to decipher its language, when he could not. As interesting and revealing as this dream was, I remained concerned that psychotherapy alone would not adequately treat this man, who had a mild to moderate manic-depressive disorder that undoubtedly would become more dramatically symptomatic with time.

Judging from the increasing amplitude and frequency of his mood swings and erratic behaviors, I knew that it was only a matter of time before Charles, untreated pharmacologically, would end up in a crisis and also in a psychiatric unit of some hospital, or worse. I continued to see him weekly, although the sessions largely consisted of his reporting on the week's events with his focus on his dwindling success in managing to function, as his mood state became more labile. I had recommended, several times, that we meet at least twice per week, but he rejected that idea, citing his inability to be out of the office so much. I thought that increasing the frequency of the sessions might settle him down a bit and would certainly give me a better gauge on his deterioration. He talked rapidly and in a circumstantial manner when he was on the high side, and with long pauses in his recitations when more depressed, but in neither case did he often respond directly to my questions, clarifications, or supportive statements. He said that he was embarrassed that at high times he spoke too rapidly for the company around him and often went off into irrelevant details, about which he was later distressed. When he was depressed, he felt lethargic, sad, and unmotivated to engage in business or in social activities. He was able to sit somewhere comfortably and stare out into the world. Although I always listened carefully for it, at no time had I heard evidence of frank psychoses; he denied being suicidal. Correctly, he read me as thinking that one of these days, he would not be able to manage, even marginally, and until then he would rather shut me out as much as possible, as if concealing the depth of his illness would avoid a complete deterioration in functioning. As with other patients I had treated in my residency program, a major crisis might have to occur for him to agree to a real trial of pharmacological treatment, which was clearly necessary to keep him on a steady functional course.

Even though a breakdown was predictable, with possible irrational, psychotic and/or suicidal behavior, there was no way to know when that would occur. It was unclear how to ensure his safety at the time, if warning was not given, as was frequently the case with patients like this. New York State law had tough commitment regulations to safeguard an individual's civil liberties, and being a possible suicidal risk at some indeterminate time did not meet the standard for involuntary hospitalization. His wife was aware of his instability and was watchful. She thought that his boss was also alerted that something was amiss with Charles. He still forbade me to talk to his wife. In our sessions, of late, Charles, feeling threatened by his lack of stability and control, also regressed to his more narcissistic, self-involved character traits. He reported that he had effectively begun isolating himself from interchange with everyone in his environment. We both recognized that he felt less stable, and I was increasingly worried that he was not entirely forthcoming during his time with me. I wondered if he had paranoid thoughts that he was not disclosing. Nonetheless, he never missed a therapy session, was entirely punctual, and I thought we had a therapeutic alliance of sorts, which would hopefully ensure that he would let me know before he did something life-threatening or nearly so.

One evening at about 10:00 p.m., I received a telephone call, at home, from Charles' wife, in which she first apologized for calling me at home at that hour and she then expressed great alarm concerning her husband. On her return from a church meeting, and coffee with friends, she had found that her husband was unexpectedly gone from their apartment, and the entire contents of the medicine chest, except for some band-aids, was missing. He left no note indicating his whereabouts. That was unusual. Even if he lied about the details, Charles always left a note or message when he had gone out unexpectedly. Her first thought was that he had taken all the leftover prescriptions, cough medicines, aspirin, and whatever else was there in order to make a suicide attempt somewhere. She reported that he had been his usual moody self during the last week, but she noted nothing more remarkable in his behavior in the last day or two. She had called the police, reported him missing, and suggested some places that he frequented when he was in distress. She mentioned two bars on Third Avenue. I advised her to check those places herself and call me from the second one if she did not locate him.

When I hung up the phone, the Lenox Hill ER immediately called to tell me that Charles Kent had wandered in there in an inebriated state, with a paper bag of assorted prescription and over-the-counter medications, crying and saying that he felt like killing himself but was afraid of what dying would feel like. He had given them my name. I hung up, called his wife – no answer and no answering machine. I ran over to Lenox Hill. Charles had not been guarded in the ER and, by the time I arrived, he had taken off while the staff responded to the consequences of a domestic gun battle. Husband and wife both had bullets in their chests. I alerted the police at the local precinct that Charles had escaped from the ER and that he was an imminent suicidal risk. At least his bag of medications had been left at the registration desk, but in his mental state, he might resort to some other means of self-destruction. I tried to reach Mrs. Kent again without success. I sat in the ER waiting room collecting my thoughts and hoping that he would again seek help before acting on his suicidal impulses.

This was the inevitable crisis I had predicted and dreaded. Unfortunately, we now knew that he was a serious suicidal risk, that he might be psychotic, and we definitely didn't have control over how this would play out. I was the likely person to take charge, I thought. I wasn't far from my residency training days and military experience when crises such as these were somewhat more regular occurrences than in private practice. I instructed the ER head nurse to continue trying to reach Mrs. Kent and have her come to Lenox Hill, which we would establish as a temporary headquarters, since when and if we found him, that would be a logical place for acute medical and psychiatric care. I also told her to leave a message for me with my office answering service, if there was any news in the next hour. I would stay in touch with the office service.

I wondered if, in his regressed state, he might seek refuge at or near my office. Although he would know that I was not planning to be there at that hour of the night, he had several times recently mentioned the comfort of my office, including joking that if he "ever needed to," he might "seek asylum" there. I ran by one of the two bars he frequented, which happened to be near my office, and found that he was not there. Confidentiality prevented me from asking questions specifically about him, but I did query the bartender about whether anyone had been there in the last hour or so who looked particularly distraught; no one had. I walked to the apartment building where my office was located, out of breath and feeling out of shape, and then ran down the hall to my office door.

Huddled in a fetal ball in a corner, at the end of the corridor, twenty feet or so from my office door, was Charles, appearing to be asleep and disheveled, with his shoe laces untied and his blue oxford shirttails half out of his pants. I quietly opened my office door and turned on the waiting room lights and then went back out to the corridor, knelt near him, and tapped on his arm and shoulder. He slowly moved and was gradually aroused by my attempts to orient him to time and place. I was not sure how long he had been asleep and why. I wondered if he had taken some of the assorted medications earlier, prior to entering the ER, or before handing them over to the triage nurse.

As soon as he was fully aware of me and the office corridor, he stood up quickly, looked frightened, his eyes darting from wall to wall to floor to various closed doors in the hallway, and said, "We must quickly get into your office, hurry. Now he might try to get both of us," he sputtered. I escorted him to my office waiting room, closed the door, and we sat down on the couch. "You've been on the run tonight, Charles. What happened?"

"Since my last session with you three days ago, I've been followed by someone who I think is going to kill me," he said, sounding strangely calm, studied. "No matter where I go, he is there, and I'm pretty sure he has a weapon. I was worried that he would also get my wife. Finally, tonight, I couldn't stand it, so I took all the medicines we have in the apartment, and I was going to kill myself before he could get me," he continued, devoid of the emotions that should have accompanied the dire circumstance he was describing. "I thought he might be satisfied with that, and then he wouldn't go after my wife. Somehow, I ended up being in the ER, and then I got frightened again by all the noise and people there, so I ran out."

"Did you take any of the pills that were in your bag?"

"No, I thought about it, but I never got around to it."

"Well, I'm glad that you didn't take a bunch of drugs that might have hurt you. Now, we can make sure that you are safe," I said. "What would help you feel more secure right now?"

"I'm not sure. Maybe we could just sit here for a little while, and you could call my wife and make sure she's all right."

I agreed to do that and reached his wife at home. I told her that Charles was with me, that he was safe, and we should all meet at Lenox Hill within the next half hour.

After about fifteen minutes, I proposed to Charles that he spend a few days in the hospital. I told him that I thought that he had been under tremendous stress, was exhausted by the evening's events and the anxiety of the last weeks, and he could benefit from some rest in a safe environment. I was firm but supportive. Charles agreed without argument and seemed finally to relax more, feeling that someone else was in charge and maybe he was not in danger from external or internal forces. I felt OK about his request to walk over to Lenox Hill with me, just a few blocks away. As we entered the ER area, I think I heard both of us breathe sighs of relief.

Charles Kent's manic-depressive disorder had followed one of the several typical courses, over the year, from mild mood swings to gradually more frequent and more dramatic variations and deterioration in functioning, and finally to psychotic thought processes, including delusions, that prevented him from accurately testing reality. Fortunately, we were able to intervene before he resorted to life-threatening behavior. As soon as I set limits on him and offered him the possibility of greater security, the psychotic symptoms diminished enough so that he was able to cooperate in the decision for treatment in a hospital setting. Although I would have preferred to have him on an involuntary certificate, in case he decided to leave precipitously, he agreed to sign in voluntarily and I did not want to feed into his paranoia by initiating a commitment procedure.

I asked that he be put on suicide and elopement precautions and requested that the ward be locked. I instructed the nurses to call me at any time if he made any statement about wanting to leave. I thought that was unlikely, at least for the next twenty-four hours, especially since I ordered a dose of a tranquilizer to be given to him in the ER, and again a few hours later, so he would sleep through the night.

Charles would need a period of stabilization in the hospital, during which time he would be started on lithium carbonate, and possibly an anti-psychotic medication, depending on how durable the paranoid delusions remained. Then, as an outpatient, he would continue the mood stabilizer indefinitely, with the option of an antidepressant and/or an antipsychotic tranquilizer, depending on the nature of his symptoms. Psychotherapy would provide at least a supportive function, possibly opening avenues for under-standing some of the developmental, family, and environmental issues which shaped him. It would also support his continuing treatment with medications and help him figure out how to function with a chronic psychiatric disorder, probably for the rest of his life.

As I feared, it took a near life-threatening crisis to help Charles Kent accept the treatment he so desperately needed. That is some-times the case with a fragile, frightened, resistant patient, regard-less of diagnosis. He seemed relieved, and he cooperated fully with the hospital program. He was discharged from the hospital after ten days and continued to see me twice weekly for three months and then weekly. He welcomed the mood stability that a medica-tion regimen brought him and used the support of psychotherapy to re-establish more normal work and home life patterns.

9.

DR. ADLER III

transference = the unconscious displacement or projection of feelings, thoughts, or wishes from childhood onto the analyst (or other people).

finally fully understood the concept of transference during the summer after I was accepted as a trainee in the analytic institute but had not yet begun classes. I had originally selected Marvin Adler because he was a senior training and supervising analyst at the Psychoanalytic Institute. Therefore, if I applied to become a candidate for psychoanalytic postgraduate training there, he would be able to continue to treat me, and I would not have to switch to another psychoanalyst on the institute faculty. Since my years of residency, I had assumed that I would go on to analytic training since that was the course followed by most of my peers in the late 1960s and early 1970s and was a genuine interest of mine at the time.

During the spring of my third year in psychoanalysis with Dr. Adler, I applied to the Institute and was interviewed by two senior analysts as a part of the admission process. I felt as though I was being examined for entrance into a secret club or fraternity. There had been the application form, the group interview with the admissions committee, the individual interviews with additional supervising analysts, and a meeting with some candidates who were on the verge of analytic "knighthood."

I never felt completely at ease with the idea of applying to the institute, although I did have enormous respect for many of my former teachers, supervisors, friends, and colleagues who had pursued that postgraduate training. In contrast to the process of finding a treating analyst, several years earlier, this experience was relatively easy. My lack of anxiety about it was testimony to the success of my personal analytic treatment thus far. I approached this venture seriously and felt that I was smart, healthy, and sufficiently motivated to join the psychoanalytic club. I felt that they should be happy to have me. I passed through the entrance procedures, and, since I had already completed several years of personal analysis, I could start classes in the fall. I felt proud that I had been selected, but, as the time approached to engage, I had an imperceptible, low-level anxiety that I could not fully explain. I was worried about the realistic commitment of time and money inherent in being a student of psychoanalysis in the Institute for several years: classes on one evening and Saturday mornings (tuition had to be paid for that); the expectation that I would continue in analysis for at least another year or two; the time and cost of two or three hours of weekly supervision for several years; the necessity of having to take on at least one, maybe two, low-fee analytic patients, who might pay just ten or twenty dollars per session for four or five hours per week. Lastly, and possibly most concerning, I dreaded the anticipated infantilization inherent in yet another formal training program of four- or five-years duration, after having already completed four years of college, four years of medical school, four years of internship and residency, and two years in the air force, where I had worked as both a general medical officer and psychiatrist. Wasn't that enough already? I was more than thirty-three years old and had just barely emerged from student status. But since this seemed like a "necessary" endeavor, with definite Talmudic overtones, which harkened back to my heritage, I forged ahead.

I went to Maine for a vacation in early August, at the home of some old family friends, hoping to have two weeks of hiking, canoeing, swimming, and sailing on and around Frye Island, in the middle of Lake Sebago, far away from New York, the Institute, my patients, and my teaching commitments. I had luxuriated in that atmosphere in other years. Even an occasional rainy day had, in past summers, provided an excuse to browse through some old antique stores and to pick up potential gifts or some old wrought iron tools which I would someday refinish. In the afternoon, I would read novels or lengthy magazine articles that I had stored up for months on my bedside table at home, never seeming to have the time or inclination to devote to them in the City. I never quite understood why the droves of New York and Boston psychiatrists flocked to the Cape, the Vineyard, or Nantucket for the weeks of August. I heard and gave enough interpretations and clarifications in my office; I did not want to overhear colleagues discussing their brilliant insights at the beach, lake, or pond. I wanted to be truly on vacation in August, and when I came to Maine, it had always seemed a long way from the shrinky life of New York.

Uncharacteristically, I could not settle into a real vacation mode that summer. In the first few days, I tried vigorously to attack all the activities available, even though it was overcast and cool. I felt a nagging discomfort. I felt disappointed that I could not relax and fully get away from my city life. I had spent several vacations with my friends, the Farbers, and I always found the natural beauty of that part of northern New England, the company, the conversation, the water sports, and the distance from Manhattan to be perfect. It was my first summer since my wife and I had separated and that may have contributed to my uneasiness, but it did not strike me as enough reason to be so distracted. The Farbers were long-term friends of mine and they had been incredibly supportive of me since the first days of our separation.

I slept fitfully, which I never did in Maine; I seemed to awaken every few hours. I remembered no dreams that would give me clues about my mental state. One morning, I thought I remembered a dream fragment in which a baby, wrapped in a blanket, was set out in a small canoe in a river or lake with his whole family watching. From my yeshiva days, I had an association to an infant Moses being put in a basket in the reeds of the Nile River, so that he would not be harmed by Pharaoh's edict that all Jewish male babies be killed. Another association was of a dead person, maybe a Native

American, being set out to sea in a boat to die. I would try to remember them to report to Dr. Adler on my return to analysis.

On the seventh day of vacation, I was seized, on awakening at 7:00 a.m., by a feeling of extreme anxiety, maybe even panic. Briefly trying to deny any psychological issues, I wondered if I could possibly have some acute thyroid problem or a cardiac arrhythmia. I quickly rejected those possibilities without any medical data. I had been tossing in bed for at least two hours, felt agitated once I sat up, and began pacing. My pulse was fast, maybe at 120, and I felt sweaty. I did not want anything to eat or drink and could not sit in one spot for more than a minute or two. Then it occurred to me in a flash – I did not want to start classes in the analytic institute in less than a month; I did not want to be a psychoanalyst. So, was that what this was all about? I thought then that I had to defer my admission or just withdraw. I felt an urgency to return to New York and speak to Dr. Adler about it immediately. I could not wait another week, even though logically nothing would happen between now and then to change my status. All the important Institute people were certainly on the Cape or the Vineyard! I was sure no one was on call for emergency admission problems of this sort. These kinds of things never happened. I can imagine that the last "emergency" at the Institute was when someone had not returned a volume of Freud's Standard Edition to the analytic library on time.

Although I had no session scheduled with Dr. Adler for more than two weeks, I would call him for an early appointment; for some reason, I thought that he might be in the City. At breakfast I told the Farbers that I had to return to New York. Even though they had both been in therapy and Saul was a physician, I did not think that they could possibly understand the real reason and the magnitude of my reaction. It seemed a little bizarre to me, and I was not sure that I understood it. They knew that I had retrieved some messages from my answering service, so I said that I had a patient emergency that the person covering for me could not resolve. That *was* the reason I was leaving, only the patient was *me*. Maybe I would explain it more fully later. I was too agitated to go into it all now and it would sound a little crazy. I just had to get going.

When I called him, I found that Dr. Adler was, indeed, in town. He seemed alarmed that I wanted to see him, and he gave me an appointment for the next morning. I left Maine and sped back to the City. Although I presumed that he was still technically on vacation, when I arrived at his office he was dressed in his usual dark suit, starched white shirt, and tie. I had taken the liberty of jeans, polo shirt, and sandals. He greeted me with an even more furrowed brow than usual. I immediately lay down on the couch and began a torrent of yelling, in fact shrieking, with intermittent sobbing, tears rolling down my cheeks, fists pounding ineffectually on the side of the couch. I am sure he thought that I had gone over the edge. I thought that was a possibility as well.

"I'm not going ahead with this; I'm not joining the Institute. It is not for me. I would be just following what everyone does without really thinking it through. They are just sheep. I am not going to be one of them. I am tired of being infantilized. I do not want to spend all that money; I don't have much. It's too much time. I have better things to do with my time. Besides, you *want* me to be an analyst. You must get credit for every analysand who signs up, or maybe, it looks bad if one of your flock *doesn't* join the Institute. I'm not signing up just to make you look good or because all your other little shrinks are doing it. I have decided I can be a successful, competent psychiatrist without all the hoopla of the Institute. I am not joining the *club*! Forget it!"

I went on like this for fifty minutes with the explosive force of a high-pressure hose. Adler said nothing during my tirade. It would have been difficult for him to do so. At the end of the session, he carefully said in his Dr. Adler way, "You are obviously very upset about the Institute and other things; we should meet again tomorrow." We set a time for tomorrow's session and I left.

In the hall outside his office, I thought to myself, *You are fucking crazy. To generate so much feeling about this, there is obviously something else going on.* That is what I would have said to a patient of mine, had he subjected me to what had just transpired. I was sweaty and hoarse; I had had a workout! I felt somewhat relieved, but I knew that this was important stuff, and I thought that maybe I was on the verge of figuring out something big. Preoccupied with my barely receding agitation and my own slightly audible mutterings, I walked past the observant doorman without word or nod.

The next day I continued with more of the same tirade against psychoanalytic training, specifically focusing on the issue of satisfying or disappointing Dr. Adler. "You expect me to follow some prescription, and I'm not going to do it just to satisfy you and your colleagues," I protested. Even I realized that this was clearly not exclusively about psychoanalytic training. I knew that even a psychiatrist in New York in the mid-1970s in the rarified environment of our profession should not get *this* upset by that decision. To engender such intense feelings, it obviously had to do with some incredibly old stuff in me and about people other than Dr. Adler, who, despite his importance in my current life, was rather new to my overall history. I was doing Dr. Adler's work (and mine), but I was too regressed on his couch to utter these ideas out loud. I also seemed not to want to let up on the "hostility" that I had revved up for him in this process. I certainly did not want to help him out. It was rare for me to allow myself such profound unbridled feelings and to act them out (or "act in," using proper psychoanalytic parlance).

When I finally settled down, toward the end of the second of these sessions, Dr. Adler said, "I don't think this is very much about the analytic institute or about my interest or stake in your training. It's about you and some old feelings."

Although I had just had those thoughts and they were obvious and incredibly simple, as Dr. Adler was wont to be in his comments, in a strange way I felt relieved to hear them from him, maybe relieved just to hear his normal calm and considered analytic voice. I realized that I feared possibly injuring him that week, in the explosion of words and the anger behind it. Maybe that is why I tried not to express anger directly at anyone, anytime.

I then remembered the dream fragments that I had in Maine, on the eve of my return to New York during the previous week. Being cast into the river, like Moses? Or a dead Indian in a canoe? I always thought that Dr. Adler sat up more alertly as I began to talk about dreams. I had chided him with the probability that this was better stuff than he usually got from other uptight shrink-patients, particularly the males in his practice. I had heard more than one analyst say that women were generally more interesting patients than men, and perhaps they got more from the experience of analysis because they often had better access to their feelings than men and were accultur-ated to talk about them more openly. In my limited psychotherapy practice experience, I felt that was true.

My associations brought me to Moses as a special child, having to fulfill extraordinary expectations and destined to do so. At the same time, he was in great danger, initially because of Pharaoh's threat to newborn Jewish males and their being cast into the River Nile, and later because he had to directly confront powerful authority figures and defiantly threaten them. He not only confronted Pharaoh but he also raged at God and, eventually, was furious with the people of Israel, at different points in the exodus from Egypt and the 40-year wandering in the desert. Although successful as a leader, Moses ultimately paid for his open expression of anger and frustration and was prevented from leading the Jews into the Promised Land.

Without prodding from Dr. Adler, this brought me to *my* being special. I was a relatively late life, unplanned, unexpected baby, seven-plus years younger than my next older sibling, my brother. I am sure that my arrival put some burden on my parents, maybe even killed them? No, not really. Partially compensating for my feelings of being somewhat unwanted, the family lore stressed how angelic and how adored I was. Maybe I was so, at least by my sisters and extended family. I am not sure I always believed it, but there is a family story, told to me by an aunt, that shortly after my birth, my sister, Cecile, then ten years old, looked at me in my bassinet with great admiration and delight and asked our mother if her new baby brother could possibly be the *Moshiach*, the Messiah. My mother reportedly said,

"It's possible." That kind of interchange was entirely possible in our family. At any rate, I always felt that I had to be as good as possible in order to be accepted. I had to perform well in as many ways as I could; I had to live up to family expectations, explicit and implicit, and there were many. My sisters were both brilliant people and my brother was smart and ambitious. I had to participate in a highly competitive family, but I also had to be angelic. I had to be a good boy. Confrontations and openly expressed anger were not permitted, at least not from me. I think that my siblings had more latitude in this area, or at least they did not shrink from the opportunities to express themselves. My sisters had great shouting matches in their teenage years over things like borrowing clothes from each other, the location of a favorite hairbrush, spending too much time in the bathroom (we only had one!) and other important issues of daily life. While political ideas, even religious beliefs, the rabbi's last sermon, were often hotly discussed and debated around our dinner table, there were implicit prohibitions of expressing angry personal thoughts and feelings.

The Institute represented an environment with expectations that I attributed to the "family" of psychiatrists – colleagues and teachers – and Dr. Adler, in particular. I had taken it on as an obligation that I thought I would have great difficulty renouncing, for fear of rejection from the "family" and being not as "successful" as I could have been. (Actually, some of my colleagues did in fact give up analytic practice along the way, even after their graduation from the Institute. They saw it as an interesting body of knowledge but did not want to have their professional lives dominated by it.) Adler was my focus of authority within the "analytic family" and it is at him that my anger for the obligation was directed. I saw him as both powerful and weak, as I did my father. Without any *real* basis, I feared retaliation from him (my father and Dr. Adler) for negative, angry emotions, and I also feared harming him, maybe even killing him with my rage. These emotions I had not consciously understood before, but they came out in my transference to Dr. Adler and in my associations to the dream fragments. I am sure that at some level I was aware, even as a young child, of my father's fragility, his potential to be hurt, and his own suppressed or repressed anger. All this reeked of Oedipal stuff that was embarrassingly apparent and right out of the psychoanalytic theory textbook; I was a bit ashamed to be so obvious. I felt that there were also more primitive elements, having to do with my feeling of Dr. Adler as a provider and nurturer whom I had to satisfy and protect to insure my survival. I realized that Moses was effectively abandoned by his mother and then cared for by his sister, Miriam, in Pharaoh's palace – another unconscious identification that I had with him. I do remember being particularly fascinated by that aspect of the Moses story.

I did not have time in the session that day to talk about the dead Indian in the canoe, except to say that it possibly had something to do with not following the path that I *should* have followed – my being cast off dead in a canoe as a punishment for something, my being excessively angry or oppositional or, again, even for my killing someone in anger. Maybe the old Indian was my dead father. Maybe the old Indian was even an old analyst! (I was just testing to see if Dr. Dr. Adler was awake.) Maybe he was the threatened lost parent. I noted that the canoe was also part of the dream's day residue, because it was the primary means of transportation around the Maine vacation island that I had just left. We would get back to all this at some point, I guessed. Dr. Adler did have an extraordinary ability to retrieve and summarize, even at a much later date, associations that I had mentioned months before, so I had no doubt that these data would also be stored by him for future use by both of us.

On the way out of the session, I felt truly buoyant, a feeling I had not had in some months. I had done a hell of a lot of analytic work that week of supposed vacation for both of us. Dr. Adler had done a little talking but mostly a lot of listening, as was the case lately. He was a great listener and I learned from him how to do that better. I felt relieved to be casting off the burden of the Institute, at least temporarily, until I fully resolved these issues. Much more importantly, I was able, through the transference to Dr. Adler, to make conscious old intrapsychic issues that had evolved because of the recent turmoil about the Institute but had been brewing unconsciously for decades. Maybe I did not have to be angelic all the time. Maybe I could get appropriately angry when I felt like it. Maybe I had exaggerated the issue of expectations on me in the first place. And if they were there, maybe I did not have to always fulfill them or suffer the consequences. What a luxury that would all be! While I understood my significant contribution to the transference, I also realized that there was a part that was contributed by Dr. Adler and my real relationship with him and the Institute. He did have that unspecified cardiac problem, so his possible vulnerability fed into my conflict, and the Institute, while having many redeeming features, *really* would be infantilizing. I *was* ambivalent about the prospect of being a baby versus a grown-up – wanting both at times. Dr. Adler would certainly say that I had not been allowed to be enough of a baby or a little boy. Stop it already! I felt like I had not had a summer vacation.

We had been through a lot in a short time, and obviously, there would be further passes over this material, as there always is in the analytic process. As I walked through the lobby, I obsessively reviewed the session in my head, feeling embarrassed about my grossly transparent expressions that *my* story, *my* dream fragments, *my* associations were *so much* more interesting than those of others of Dr. Adler's patients, my siblings – all evidence of my insecurity about status within the "family," large and small. And such competitiveness! My identification with Moses was indeed a bit grandiose. He had always been one of my most admired biblical characters, exhibiting such a complex character, being both monumentally heroic and also so humanly vulnerable.

I could not stop analyzing this material as I walked down the street and as I tried to attend to my other duties of the day. It obviously had stirred up a deep well of old feelings, but I had to reenter the real world. I had to focus on other things, including a few remaining days of vacation in the City. The doorman had nodded as I left the building; I waved back absent-mindedly. I am sure he knew when one of the building's analysands had an important breakthrough. *Ha ha*, I thought, whoever doubted the existence of the unconscious.

10.

DR. ADLER IV

" In the dream, I was driving around the Upper East Side of Manhattan, in the area between about 88th and 96th Streets, and maybe between Lexington Avenue and the East River. That is our old family stomping grounds, as you know. I was driving the blue Fiat I now own, appeared to be my current age, but I felt oddly childlike – timid, fragile, and insecure. In the back seat of the car was a small solid oak or walnut plain bench or stool, about eighteen to twenty-four inches long, with a keyhole handgrip cut out in the middle of the seat, possibly for easy carrying. It was similar, a bit taller than the kind of stool that I remember sitting on in the children's sections of the old public libraries that we frequented in Manhattan. We could also use them to step up to reach books on higher shelves. In the dream I thought of the bench as a valuable antique. Then, at times in the dream, I was not in the car, but rather, suddenly darting into some stores and into several brownstone houses, typical of that neighborhood, and frantically asking the people in those places if they had seen my car. I had apparently parked it somewhere on one of the nearby streets, off Third Avenue or Lexington, and then I couldn't find it. I wondered whether it had been stolen. I was upset by that possibility, especially since the valuable antique bench in the back seat would be lost with the car. I felt sad that what I thought was a fine family heirloom might have been stolen, along with my Fiat. My anxiety mounted as time passed. It was getting toward evening, and I could not locate the car, and maybe more importantly, the bench inside it. Distraught, almost in a panic, I frenetically darted into more of the brownstones. Finally, miraculously, I happened upon my car on one of the nearby side streets. Relieved, I woke up." In telling the dream to Dr. Adler, I talked fast and again experienced some of the agitation I had felt in the dream.

"So, what do you think about it?" Dr. Adler asked.

"The bench looked like it belonged in one of those old Andrew Carnegie funded New York Public Libraries. There was one on 96th Street, off Lexington Avenue. We used to often walk there sometimes from my grandparents' house on *Shabbat*. I must have been six to eight years old and I'd always go with one of my sisters and my brother. I would get tired on the way home, and they would make fun of me, teasing that we were going to take the long way home. Walks to the library on *Shabbat* were important rituals in our family. Because it was *Shabbat,* we didn't transact any business in the library; we just browsed among the books and I sometimes read one there. There was something very precious about those days and those walks. They were peaceful, calm. I felt close to my brother and sisters. There was a minimum of teasing. They had to do at least a bit of it; it was their job!

"In losing the valuable stool, and that seemed more significant than the car, I felt childlike, worried, desperately so. I had lost something especially important. Oh shit, not that again."

"It keeps coming up, doesn't it?" Dr. Adler said, in a supportive tone that emphasized one of the major themes of my analysis, and possibly my life, to that point. Now I was near the end of the analysis, and yet I was still reviewing the old feelings of loss, even if mostly in dreams.

"It was a familiar anxiety feeling in the dream, that 'pit of my stomach' feeling. The neighborhood was Yorkville, my maternal grandparents' neighborhood, where I had lived, on the third floor of their brownstone in fact, for the first five years of my life, and where we regularly visited afterwards until my grandmother's death. I surely associate 89th Street and Yorkville, in general, with the maternal side of the family, with my maternal grandparents, and by extension, with my mother. It was also the home base for my extended family during my growing-up years, even until I was past thirty. It was the celebratory gathering place for the family. We had moved to the Bronx by the time my mother had her mastectomy. Did I ever tell you that both my mother and maternal grandmother died on the same day on the Hebrew calendar, the eve of Passover, thirty-five years apart?"

"Yes, you've mentioned it a few times," Dr. Adler said. "In a way, you lost two mothers on the eve of Passover, so it's not surprising that it continues to be a memorable day for you. We are close to that anniversary."

"I've always thought that I get slightly anxious, as Passover approaches. The anniversary never escapes me, and a month or so before, I want to be sure of our plans to have a *Seder,* within the family or with friends. As soon as plans are confirmed, the anxiety recedes. *Why is this night different from all other nights?* It is obvious!

"Various of my family members put a great deal of significance on the fact that both my mother and her mother died on the same day on the Jewish calendar." I continued, "Especially since my grandmother, at 103 years of age, could have died on any day over many years. An aunt of mine expressed the idea that since my grandmother was so close to my mother, her eldest child, and never got over her death, she 'chose' or she "was fated" to die on the same day. I guess that my repeating things like this shows that it is time to terminate the analysis – ha, ha, ha.

"Back to my dream, my search was frenzied, looking for someone to help me find the car, and especially, the stool. I also thought of the carved hole in the seat as another symbol of something missing. My loss, so many years later, transposed into a lost wooden stool, an antique (primitive stuff) and something of great value to me and my family. Where it *really* belonged was behind me, as in the back seat of the car. And, thankfully, that is where it was again when I finally found the car.

"I just thought that, of course, the bench also looked a lot like the ones the undertakers brought to the house for the week of *shiva.* I remember those being in our house after my mother died. I wonder if they still use those heavy wooden benches. I remember them as being solid, maybe oak or walnut. No, now they are undoubtedly made of plastic. "This stuff doesn't go away, and I'm reworking it, but I really feel on top of it now; I know the drill. I feel as though this dream is, in a way, a summary of the analysis, with the emphasis on loss and recovery, and hopefully, some mastery," I added.

"Losses and their scars are definitely a part of you, and it may not ever fully go away. You also have many strengths, partially, at least, gained from the solid family that reliably supported you through difficult times (that solid oak or walnut bench) and celebrated the joyful ones. You are reviewing all of it, maybe even more so as you prepare to finish here, and you do have a much better grasp on how profoundly your history has affected you. The consequences now are quite limited, but you continue to work over the feelings and memories, and still mourn, at least in your dreams," Dr. Adler offered.

"And now, why did the dream occur last night?" I continued. "Maybe a contribution was a patient I saw yesterday who talked about the scars of terrible loss – hiding from the Nazis in wartime Prague and then, when able to come out of the hiding place provided by a Christian family, having to live under the Russian-controlled Czech Communist regime. Finally, she and her family decided to leave everything behind, to literally throw the key to the house away, into the Vlatava, and with forged papers escape to Vienna and eventually to New York. She cried as she was telling the story, more than twenty-five years later, evoked the raw pain of those years. I was moved both by the poignant story and the strength and resilience which emanated from the woman and her frail torso, thin wrinkled face, and sad, but, I suspected, once sparkling, eyes. I guess that she also reminded me of my grandmother, who did not personally live through the horrors of the 1930s and '40s in Europe but nonetheless felt the pain of her generation because of family and friends left behind in Zlochev, all of whom were killed by the Nazis in the Holocaust. My grandmother had a special ability to cope, no matter what the stress or provocation, including experiencing the death of her eldest child, my mother, at a relatively young age.

"So, it all falls together. The blue Fiat represents me now, and those antique, old, even primitive, feelings are tucked away in my back seat but occasionally get stirred up and become disruptive, evoking early childhood experiences and emotions. Thankfully, lately, they have mostly come up in occasional dreams, rather than upsets in my daily life. I certainly feel much more resilient than I ever have. I credit my work with you, and, secondarily, my being able to simultaneously recognize and work through similar issues that recur repeatedly with my patients."

"I agree," Dr. Adler remarked. "And so, what does the dream have to do with us?"

"It just popped into my head. I just realized, and I know that our time is up, that the search for and discovery of the car and the stool in the neighborhood of my early childhood, also is in **your** neighborhood, not only relates to my old history but is a metaphor for the analysis. The *shiva* reference to the bench, I think, also must have something to do with you. I am surely mourning the ending of this relationship, ending my analysis, which I have joked about lately. I have tried to search for something that was lost, to remember, mourn, recover, and move on. I was looking for someone to help me find what I had lost. What a great dream! OK, I am ready to stop. I have a handle on the old narratives.

"This analysis will end soon," I continued, not waiting for, and maybe not wanting, Dr. Adler's comments, wondering whether this was the way it was supposed to end. "I will live my life without the luxury of having you to listen to my daily minutia, and without going with the associations, and most of all, without your commentary and interpretation. Can you imagine, I will live the rest of my life without all of that, except what I generate myself? Analysis has, at times, felt very self-indulgent, but it also felt like a necessity for several of those years. I have learned so much about what makes me tick and, most importantly, about how to do this work on my own. We have not said anything specifically about my terminating, but I am ready and a bit anxious about that prospect. I owe you a great debt."

It is difficult to be a patient and a psychiatrist – knowing a lot about the process, theoretically and practically, but also often second-guessing it and having some difficulty surrendering control. I marveled at how my associations, dreams, thoughts, and ramblings consistently pointed to the same set of narratives in my history. I was about to leave Dr. Adler's building for one of the last times, and then I realized that I had left a book I had carried into the session, on the floor next to the couch in his office. With some embarrassment, I quickly turned around, ran up to his office before his next patient arrived, retrieved it, and headed out again.

AFTERWORD

"We have to deal with our necessary losses. We should under-stand how these losses are linked to our gains." (Judith Viorst, *Necessary Losses*, Simon and Schuster, 1986)

In looking back at the early years of my work with patients in psychotherapy and since, I am struck by the idea that all of us, patients and psychotherapists, have threads of history and personal narrative that start early in our lives and follow us throughout our development as individuals, even into old age. Many of those threads, hopefully, are useful, productive, healthy, and meaningful. Some, unfortunately, are painful, destructive, even dangerous to well-being and happiness. In most people, there is usually a mixture of these. In my studies and in my work, I have seen that psychotherapeutic treatment can have a significant impact on people who want to, or must, sort out and understand the threads of their lives so that they can, hopefully, live more successfully and happily. It has been important to me to have engaged in that process, both as an analytic patient and as a therapist. It is not suited for everyone, nor for every psychological problem, but psychoanalytic or psychodynamic psychotherapy can be a valuable modality, even as other treatments have become more available, less costly, and less time intensive.

I have focused a great deal in this book on the effects of loss and mourning, aspects of life which most of us experience at some points in our lives, aspects with which many of us have considerable difficulty, if they are not fully examined. The losses may be of varied origins and may be compounded by multiple causes. They may include losses of important people whom we had hoped we would have in our lives forever or at least for a long time, as was the case in my life and that of Mrs. Gold's. They may be losses of hoped-for opportunities for idealized, or at least better, experiences or relationships with significant people, as was the case with Mr. Weiss, Ms. Burns, and Mr. Kent. They may entail losses of self-esteem that reduce effectiveness in living life, as with several of the people I have described here. There are often losses of physical and/or emotional attributes or strengths, which we once possessed but, because of age or infirmity, have diminished. These are losses which Mrs. Gold and Mr. Weiss felt and about which they talked in therapy. Lastly, there are losses of eras of our lives, which because of normal development, we must give up in going on to next steps. About these we may be wistful, having warm reminiscences at best, or mournful, largely because other aspects of life have not been fulfilling or because we have not built up a sufficient reserve of psychological strengths.

In whatever form they take, the losses in our lives are best realized, confronted, and then mourned, so that they become memories, possibly even adding to our strengths through mastery and resilience, rather than determinants of our negative feelings, thoughts, and future life paths. The process of uncovering, beginning to feel, and then untangling the losses in our lives can be a difficult one, but it is essential, if we are going to be mentally healthy, that we spend the effort, time, and energy, and sometimes, feel the pain that causes. Mourning of this kind does not usually follow a predictable timetable or pattern and may have to be done over years, even decades, sometimes continuously, sometimes more intermittently, depending on life circumstances.

I returned briefly to see Dr. Adler seven and fifteen years after I "completed" my analysis, to cope better with the feelings generated by the untimely death of my brother and then the deaths of my two sisters, both of which occurred within a short period. Those sets of sessions, over several months each, were useful "boosters," which allowed me to deal with the losses of my three siblings at unexpected times. I needed to fully mourn and remind myself of the complicated feelings that were provoked by those losses and those from my past. Mrs. Gold worked on mourning several significant people in her life, and earlier themes, intermittently for seven years, until well into her eighties, with me and then with other therapists after her move to another city. Ms. Burns intermittently suffered with the traumas of her early life for decades with increasing ability to separate old narratives of her childhood and adolescence from whom she was as a high functioning adult. She worked to repair "the hole" she felt from her earliest days. Mr. Weiss's life, and his work with me, were unfortunately cut short by his illness and death, but I believe that he gained from our time together, partially because he had begun to mourn his missed opportunities and relationships in his previous treatment with other therapists. Although he came to better appreciate his significant strengths, many issues remained unresolved. Mr. Kent continued in treatment with me sporadically for more than ten years. He was mostly diligent in following a prescribed mood-stabilizing medication regimen and coped better with aspects of his chronic mood disorder so that he could function relatively well. He came to better terms with his expectations, limitations, and successes.

ACKNOWLEDGEMENTS

My wife, Gail, suggested the title of this book. For that, and her support, advice and patience over the years, I am very grateful. I appreciate the encouragement that Ann Epstein and Bernard Edelstein offered when they read an early version of the manuscript, and their continuing support during the years as it matured into a book. I also am grateful to Steve Epstein, Richard Waldhorn, Jane Stine, Nancy Sherman, and Beverly Nadel for reading the manuscript at various stages of its development and for giving me helpful comments. Linda Cashdan, Linda Carbone, and Michelle Brafman offered essential editing along the way.